THE
CREATIVE WRITER'S
NOTEBOOK

METRO BOOKS
New York

An Imprint of Sterling Publishing
1166 Avenue of the Americas
New York, NY 10036

Conceived, designed, and produced by
Quid Publishing
Level 4 Sheridan House
114 Western Road
Hove BN3 1DD
England

Design by Rehabdesign

www.quidpublishing.com

ISBN: 978-1-4351-6018-7

For information about custom editions, special sales,
and premium and corporate purchases, please contact
Sterling Special Sales at 800-805-5489
or specialsales@sterlingpublishing.com.

Manufactured in China

1 3 5 7 9 10 8 6 4 2

www.sterlingpublishing.com

THE CREATIVE WRITER'S NOTEBOOK

A Creative Journal for Fiction Writers

John Gillard

METRO BOOKS
New York

CONTENTS

JAMES JOYCE

Born: February 2, 1882

Died: January 13, 1941

Writing: Modernist

Key work: *Ulysses*

J ames Joyce is arguably the most influential writer of the twentieth century. His masterpiece, *Ulysses* (1922), challenged the traditional rules of style and form and changed the landscape of modern literature.

Genesis of Ideas

Dublin, Ireland, was always the center of Joyce's stories. He was born in the city in 1882, yet left for continental Europe at the age of 22, never to return to live there. Despite living in Trieste, Paris, and Zurich, and only sporadically returning to visit his home city, he wrote precise and detailed descriptions of the streets and alleyways of Dublin, particularly in *Ulysses*. He said: "For myself, I always write about Dublin, because if I can get to the heart of Dublin I can get to the heart of all the cities of the world. In the particular is contained the universal." Like the work of all great writers, Joyce's stories resonate with everyone. Although they may seem inconsequential, merely events of a single day, they are universal.

The genesis of Joyce's literary ideas and innovative style spanned the years from his first publication at the age of 18—a review of Henrik Ibsen's dreamlike *When We Dead Awaken* (1899), at which point he learned basic Norwegian in order to send a fan-letter to Ibsen—through to an early autobiographical essay, *Portrait of the Artist as a Young Man* (1904) and onto *Ulysses* and *Finnegans Wake* (1939).

Brimming with Confidence

Portrait of the Artist in its first form was rejected for publication. In the same year Joyce revised it into a novel called *Stephen Hero* but abandoned it. Joyce's work was evolving. The character, Stephen Hero, was now an alter ego of Joyce himself and would later become Stephen Dedalus, who, along with Leopold Bloom, was the main character in *Ulysses*. *Portrait of the Artist* was rewritten as *A Portrait of the Artist as a Young Man* and published 12 years after its original conception. It was Joyce's first published novel. This time it was brimming with confidence. In *Portrait* Joyce introduced Stephen Dedalus (Daedalus is the craftsman

Joyce's direct influence on other writers has been huge; we can see it in William Faulkner's stream of consciousness, in the interior monologues of Gabriel García Márquez, and in Raymond Queneau's multiple telling of the same story in different styles.

‹ James Joyce in conversation with the publishers of *Ulysses* in the famous bookshop Shakespeare and Co.

father of Icarus in Greek mythology) and used the device of interior monologue to bring the reader into Stephen's developing consciousness. The stream-of-consciousness language mirrors Stephen's intellectual maturing: "moocow" evolving to "the uncreated conscience of my race." Joyce would take this style even further in his next novel, his masterpiece *Ulysses*.

The events of *Ulysses* occur on a single day, June 16, 1904, yet the novel is 265,000 words in length. The complex and seemingly chaotic structure is broken into 18 episodes that trace the story of Homer's *Odyssey*. Joyce's use of streams of consciousness is taken to new levels with the final episode. The interior monologue of Molly Bloom is 4,391 words long, almost entirely unpunctuated: "...I was a Flower of the mountain yes when I put the rose in my hair like the Andalusian girls used or shall I wear a red yes and how he kissed me under the Moorish Wall and I thought well as well him as another...."

T. S. Eliot said of *Ulysses*: "I hold this book to be the most important expression which the present age has found; it is a book to which we are all indebted, and from which none of us can escape." Joyce's contemporary, William Faulkner, said, "You should approach Joyce's *Ulysses* as the illiterate Baptist preacher approaches the Old Testament: with faith." A reading of *Ulysses*, for all its complexity, is invaluable to an aspiring writer. It paved the way for future generations to experiment and innovate and, along with authors such as Faulkner, Ernest Hemingway, and Virginia Woolf, ushered in the modernist era.

"...the modern writer must be an adventurer... we must write dangerously."

—James Joyce, in
Conversations with James Joyce by Arthur Power

INTERIOR MONOLOGUE:
YOURSELF

The interior monologue is the thought process of a character written from their perspective. A method of writing an interior monologue is through "stream of consciousness," allowing any conscious thought that comes to mind to be written down. In stream-of-consciousness mode, sentence structure and style need not be considered during the process of writing.

Exercise: Write an interior monologue using stream of consciousness from your own perspective (ie, write down the flow of your own conscious thoughts). You might like to use Joyce's method of writing without punctuation, with each thought a continuation of the last, until you reach the end of the page. Is this a method of writing you would like to develop so as to allow you and your readers to get into the mind of the characters?

Date

FINNEGANS WAKE

In *Finnegans Wake* James Joyce uses an incredible amount of wordplay. He enjoyed creating portmanteau words—a single word with two meanings. The word derives from the English term "portmanteau luggage"— a piece of luggage with two compartments. An example of a portmanteau from *Finnegans Wake* is "kissmiss": both an alternative spelling of "Christmas" and something that may occur under the mistletoe.

Exercise: Try to come up with some portmanteaus of your own. A few examples are given below to help.

> "Mr. Right" (A man's name and his suitability)
> "Kissmiss"
> "Eleventeen" (A mature eleven-year-old)
> "Smog" (Smoke and fog)

FAMILY MEMBERS

Pick members of your family and write a description of them using their age as your word count (eg, Nana, 71, Dad, 48, your niece, Lucy, 5). Could you think of a single word to describe your one-year-old baby nephew? Mix up the descriptions so that your paragraph has varying sentence lengths. Mixing up short and long sentences helps to structure prose and varies the pace.

VIRGINIA WOOLF

Born: January 25, 1882

Died: March 28, 1941

Writing: Modernist

Key works: *Orlando*; *A Room of One's Own*

Virginia Woolf is the foremost feminist writer of the twentieth century. With her mastery of the interior monologue and stream of consciousness she is one of the key figures in the development of modernist literature.

Interior Monologue

In her novels Woolf tears up previously accepted structures of narration. Instead, she mixes narration with her characters' inner voice. Rather than the traditional narrator telling us what happens next, we hear how characters react to what happens. Woolf ushers the reader into the characters' minds, while retaining the narrative layer. "Yes, he did say disagreeable things, Mrs. Ramsay admitted; it was odious of him to rub this in…" (*To the Lighthouse*; 1927). Here the word "yes" leads us into the character's thoughts. Then we have the narrator coming in, organizing and distinguishing for us. The semicolon then reintroduces the flow of thoughts. Woolf skillfully balances stream of consciousness with punctuation, so that the underlying meaning comes through to the reader.

Through interior monologue Virginia Woolf explores the psychological and emotional motives of her characters. Much has been written about Woolf's own psychology and mental illness and about the manner of her death: how she filled her pockets with stones and walked into the River Ouse. Her mental instability was a lifelong affliction and it often affected her social life, though it did not appear to stifle her work; she was prolific in her output. She explored a great variety of genres: novels, nonfiction books, short-story collections, biographies, autobiographical writings, and diaries.

Woolf married in 1912 and set up the Hogarth Press with her husband, Leonard. They were able to publish Woolf's novels themselves. They also published works by T. S. Eliot, among others. This contrasted sharply with the problems of publication experienced by her contemporary and fellow modernist, James Joyce.

Margaret Atwood's novel *Oryx and Crake* (2003) starts with an epigraph quoting Woolf's *To the Lighthouse*. Its main character, Snowman, lists great human achievements, which include the complete works of Shakespeare, heart transplants, and Virginia Woolf.

‹ Woolf at her home, Monk's House, in Sussex, England.

"Going at such a pace as I do I must make the most direct shots at my object...with no more pause than is needed to put my pen in the ink."

—Virginia Woolf, *A Writer's Diary*

Woolf's sister, Vanessa, and her husband, Clive Bell, both avant-garde artists, had an important influence on Woolf's development as an author. The two couples became part of the Bloomsbury Set, a group of intellectuals who were united by their belief in the value of the arts.

Orlando

The liberal avant-garde style of the Bloomsbury group was reflected in their approach to sexuality. In 1922 Virginia Woolf met the writer and gardener Vita Sackville-West and they began a sexual relationship. Sackville-West was the inspiration for Woolf's groundbreaking novel *Orlando* (1928), a mix of satirically historical biography and exploration of gender roles. Orlando is a young nobleman in Elizabethan England. At the age of 30 he falls asleep for a week. When he awakes he finds he has metamorphosed into a woman, yet his mind and personality remain the same. Woolf again experiments with the narrator. While Orlando, living in a different age and gender, appears unconcerned, the narrator is disturbed.

Woolf's language is intensely lyrical. She creates a world full of auditory and visual impressions: "How fresh, how calm, stiller than this of course, the air was in the early morning; like the flap of a wave; the kiss of a wave; chill and sharp and yet (for a girl of eighteen as I then was) solemn…" (*Mrs. Dalloway*; 1925). The reader feels what the character is experiencing; the words "flap" and "kiss" give the sound and the touch of the air, comparing it in our imagination with a wave. She wrote, "Yet, it is true, poetry is delicious; the best prose is that which is most full of poetry."

Virginia Woolf said diaries brought freedom to her writing; "…it loosens the ligaments." Like the cliché "dance like nobody is watching," writing something that nobody else will read, in stream of consciousness, allows you to write with complete freedom. This freedom can be practiced and makes for better writing.

Exercise: Try Woolf's method of free writing. Use these pages of the notebook to write your thoughts on whatever subject you like. Don't worry about spelling or grammar, or how it reads—you don't even need to read it back yourself. As Woolf said, "Never mind the misses and the stumbles." Is this something you would like to take further and practice every day in a writing journal?

POINT OF VIEW

It is important to write effectively from different viewpoints. In *Orlando* Virginia Woolf writes from both the male and female perspective within the same character.

Exercise: A man is sitting at a table on his own in a crowded Italian restaurant. A woman from another table gets up, walks over to his table, and sits down opposite him. Write three versions of the same scene from three different perspectives.

Write this scene in the first person from the perspective of one of the characters.
(eg, *I can see her looking at me in the reflection of the glass...*)

Write this scene in the third person.
(eg, *She picked up her glass of wine...*)

Write dialogue between them.

LITTLE DAILY MIRACLES

Write a short piece using the following line from Woolf's *To the Lighthouse* for inspiration:

"Little daily miracles"

FRANZ KAFKA

Born: July 3, 1883

Died: June 3, 1924

Writing: Modernist; existentialism

Key work: *The Metamorphosis*

F ranz Kafka changed the face of modern literature. Largely unpublished in his own lifetime, he paved the way for future writers to shock, surprise, and push boundaries.

A Creative Outpouring

"As Gregor Samsa awoke one morning from uneasy dreams he found himself transformed in his bed into a gigantic insect." The opening line of Kafka's *The Metamorphosis* (1915) was revolutionary in its bold absurdity. It had a profound influence on a young Gabriel García Márquez (*One Hundred Years of Solitude*): "The first line almost knocked me off the bed. I was so surprised…I thought to myself that I didn't know anyone was allowed to write things like that." *The Metamorphosis* changed the face of what a story could be—the metaphorical breakdown of body and mind is portrayed with such original absurdity. Samsa's surreal transformation is set against reality. He increasingly disgusts his family and he can no longer communicate even though his mind is still human. This existential nightmare set new ground for the modernist movement.

Despite his enormous influence on the literary world, Kafka was never aware of the impact of his work during his lifetime. He published only one collection of stories and a few stories in literary magazines. In fact we may have seen only a fraction of his overall output. He is said to have burned 90% of his work, and many of his notebooks and letters remain unseen having been confiscated by the Gestapo in 1933. One particular story published in his lifetime had a huge impact on the evolution of his writing. *The Judgment* (1912) is seen as his breakthrough work. It deals with the troubled relationship of a son and dominant father, a theme that would run throughout his work, both explicitly and metaphorically. He wrote the story in a single night. He described this creative outpouring as "a complete opening of body and soul." In a prolific year Kafka also wrote *The Metamorphosis* and the novel *The Man Who Disappeared*, published posthumously in 1927 as *Amerika*.

"My doubts stand in a circle around every word, I see them before I see the word, but what then! I do not see the word at all, I invent it."

—Franz Kafka,
Diaries: 1910–1923

Fearless

Kafka's apparent lack of confidence in his work showed itself in a letter to his lifelong friend, Max Brod: "Dearest Max, my last request: Everything I leave behind me ... in the way of diaries, manuscripts, letters (my own and others'), sketches, and so on, [is] to be burned unread." Brod ignored his friend and took them to publication. Kafka's masterpieces, *Amerika*, *The Trial* (1925), and *The Castle* (1926), all unfinished, were published after his death, cementing his place in literary history.

In an extract from his diary Kafka said, "[I would] rather tear myself to a thousand pieces than be buried with this world within me." He poured his feelings of inadequacy and isolation into his stories. He tore into the over-bearing power of faceless bureaucracy. In another diary entry he described the writer inside him as "fearless, powerful, surprising, moved...." Kafka worked for The Worker's Accident Insurance Institute all his adult life, largely to please his father. Rather than curtailing his creativity, it seemed only to fuel it further. His day job was certainly a source for his characters. Would he have written *The Metamorphosis* and the character of

▲ A page from Franz Kafka's diary, showing the author's own sketches accompanying his text.

Kafka's treatment of the surreal in his novella *The Metamorphosis* prefigured the magical realism of works such as Haruki Murakami's *Kafka on the Shore* (2002).

Gregor Samsa, traveling salesman transformed, without the anxieties and frustrations he felt within his own job? Through the surreal, through darkness, unease, humor, and shock, he spoke of universal human struggles. As W. H. Auden once wrote, "Kafka is important to us because his predicament is the predicament of modern man."

THE CREATIVE WRITER'S NOTEBOOK   25

Can you come up with a killer first line? A line to shock, intrigue, or frame an entire story? Here is Gabriel García Márquez's opening line in *One Hundred Years of Solitude*: "Many years later, as he faced the firing squad, Colonel Aureliano Buendía was to remember that distant afternoon when his father took him to discover ice."

Exercise: Take a piece of your writing or a story you have considered, or are planning to write. Or create a new idea for a story. Try to write an opening line with impact, which will lead the reader straight into the story, and inform them of what might be to come.

JUXTAPOSITION

Putting together images or thoughts that are not normally associated will create juxtapositions that remain in the reader's mind. For example: a homeless man wearing a weathered tuxedo.

Exercise: Make a note here of anything strange and unusual, weird and wonderful, that you see, hear, smell, read, taste, or touch. In your notes begin to look for connections. Put together disconnected images that juxtapose. Form similes and metaphors. Look out for new characters and character descriptions.

In the following description there is a strong feeling of a writer noting down the facts of a man and his life. The writer is present to the reader. The only presence should be the characters in the story; the writer's voice should be implicit.

Character: A traveling salesman. He is 193cm. He has a bad back because he spends so many nights sleeping in cheap hotels with uncomfortable beds. He is divorced and has two young children, a boy and a girl.

Exercise: Take these facts and write them into a description of the character that is revealed through actions and strong narration and/or dialogue.

Character: A doctor. She is married and has a one-year-old baby boy. Her husband is a stay-at-home dad. She has just finished a 20-hour shift and is beginning to hallucinate.

Exercise: Take these facts and write them into a description of the character that is revealed through actions and strong narration and/or dialogue.

WILLIAM FAULKNER

Born: September 25, 1897

Died: July 6, 1962

Writing: Modernist; Southern gothic

Key work: *The Sound and the Fury*

W illiam Faulkner is one of the great American modernist writers. In his portrayal of Deep South America, he experimented with structure and style, using streams of consciousness, multiple perspectives, and distorted chronology.

Yoknapatawpha

Like his contemporary, Ernest Hemingway, Faulkner broke away from any established rules and conventions of writing. Where Hemingway broke the rules with brevity and omission, Faulkner used streams of consciousness and interior monologue, influenced by James Joyce and Thomas Mann. Faulkner inhabited the characters he portrayed and spoke in their voices. He wrote with the diction of the Deep South, changing the rhythm, cadence, and grammar of his prose to fit the character—poor or rich, cerebral or simple, or verging on insanity: "Sometimes I think it aint none of us pure crazy and aint none of us pure sane until the balance of us talks him that-a-way. It's like it aint so much what a fellow does, but it's the way the majority of folks is looking at him when he does it" (*As I Lay Dying*; 1930).

Faulkner created the fictional setting of Yoknapatawpha County to house his stories and characters, based on his childhood surroundings in Mississippi. Yoknapatawpha is populated with outsiders, eccentrics, runaway slaves, formerly rich white plantation owners, and drifters consumed by mixed ancestry. Through these characters Faulkner writes about social class, race, sex (and incest), and the human effects of a changing society.

What Is the Truth?

Faulkner uses distorted chronology and multiple narratives to question ideas of history and truth. Our present is the sum of our past, or more importantly our perception of our past. To Faulkner the past coexists with the present. He often tells a story in the present and then takes us back to see the story again from a point in the past. In the opening of *Absalom, Absalom!* (1936) we are told the

JOHN GILLARD

Faulkner's short story *A Rose for Emily* (1930) is often held up as a classic example of Southern gothic, taking elements of the gothic genre of Mary Shelley and Edgar Allan Poe: grotesque acts, decaying mansions, and suspense.

‹ Faulkner's Underwood typewriter, in the office where he did much of his writing.

rags-to-riches story of Thomas Sutpen. Three narrators then recount his story through the novel, each giving a different interpretation. This act of storytelling using streams of consciousness, filling in any gaps with beliefs and opinions, gives the story a mythlike quality, blurring the line between truth and folklore: "...that alertness for measuring and weighing event against eventuality, circumstance against human nature, his own fallible judgment and mortal clay against not only human but natural forces, choosing and discarding, compromising with his dream and his ambition like you must with the horse which you take across country, over timber...." We are left to question what the real truth of the story is, or even if there is one truth, since history is governed by perspectives. This blurring of myth and reality would influence the magical realism of Gabriel García Márquez, Salmon Rushdie, and Haruki Murakami.

Faulkner was a prolific writer. He wrote 15 novels set in Yoknapatawpha. His writing was often brisk. In an introduction to his novel *Sanctuary* (1932) Faulkner describes writing *As I Lay Dying* (1930), narrated by 15 characters, in six weeks, between the hours of midnight and 4am, without changing a single word. The critic Harold Bloom said of the book: "It seems to me an authentic instance of the literary sublime in our time."

Faulkner's dense, complex novels might require the reader to sit down with a strong black coffee or stiff bourbon. In an interview with *The Paris Review* in 1958, Faulkner showed his confident, wry humor:

INTERVIEWER: Some people say they can't understand your writing, even after they read it two or three times. What approach would you suggest for them?
FAULKNER: Read it four times.

"Read! You'll absorb it. Then write. If it is good, you'll find out. If it's not, throw it out of the window."
—William Faulkner, Statement at the University of Mississippi, 1947

AN AUTHENTIC VOICE

William Faulkner wrote in streams of consciousness, inhabiting his characters and allowing them to speak freely. If his characters repeated words and spoke with broken grammar, then this is how he would write them. His sentences are long and full of subordinate clauses:

"Or maybe it's women that dont need reasons, for the simple reason that they never heard of a reason and wouldn't recognise it face to face, since they dont function from reasons but from necessities that couldn't nobody help nohow and that dont nobody but a fool man want to help in the second place, because he dont know no better; it aint women, it's men that takes ignorance seriously, getting into a skeer over something for no more reason than that they dont happen to know what it is." The repetitive use of the word "reason" gives a unique cadence to the character's voice, a pulsing beat, and a sense of his simple nature.

Exercise: Put yourself into the mind of a character who has a unique voice. This can be a person you know, someone chosen from the movies or television, or you can create your own character. Write an interior monologue recounting a story, or talking about a subject of your choosing (real or imagined), or from the prompts on the following page. Allow the words and grammar to fit the manner and nature of the person you inhabit.

Prompts:

You are walking along a dusty road. In the distance, you see a woman walking toward you. As she passes you, she says nothing, but hands you a letter from her late husband and walks on.

You are stuck in a traffic jam, with the sun beaming down and the air conditioning broken.

Drinking black coffee in a roadside café. There is no milk or sugar.

Date

012

CROSSING THE RIVER

Dialogue drives story and character development. It brings the reader into the heart of things. Great dialogue also looks good on the page. Story without dialogue can be heavy and lacking in color and texture.

Exercise: Two people are discussing how to get to the other side of a river with no obvious way across. Write a passage of dialogue between these two people. They have strong colloquial diction. Imagine the sound of their voices and write the dialogue so that the reader can interpret the diction and hear their voices. Allow yourself the freedom to tear the words up. Keep the treatment of words consistent and ensure they remain legible and coherent. For this exercise keep all the dialogue qualifiers simple (eg, "he said" and "she said"). Don't use any adverbs to qualify the dialogue such as "she said angrily." Instead, show the reader the anger in the voice from what is said and how it is said.

In the course of their dialogue what can the reader find out about the characters? Perhaps the dialogue carries them to the other side of the river? Or perhaps they end up talking about something completely different?

013

INSPIRATION FROM
THE ART WORLD

William Faulkner was influenced by the work of modernist painters such as Pablo Picasso and Georges Braque. They experimented with varying perspectives of a single subject within a painting, just as Faulkner experimented with multiple narratives and the unreliable narrator.

Exercise: Write a short piece inspired by a painting, sculpture, or any other form of artwork of your choosing. Think about the senses evoked within the artwork—the sounds, the tastes, the smells. What are the stories behind painted objects or people? Do any abstract forms trigger your own abstract thoughts and memories?

ERNEST HEMINGWAY

Born: July 21, 1899

Died: July 2, 1961

Writing: Modernist

Key work: *Fiesta: The Sun Also Rises*

E rnest Hemingway is one of the great American writers. He discarded traditional rules of form and style and was pivotal in the emergence of modernism. He is arguably the most influential writer of the twentieth century.

The Iceberg

Hemingway is known for the brevity of his writing and his ability to say things without actually saying them. He believed that writing should be like an iceberg, in the sense that, above the waterline, only one-eighth of an iceberg is seen. In *Out of Season* (1923) Hemingway omitted the "real" ending (the old man, Peduzzi, hanging himself) because he believed omission was not only possible but actually benefited the story. The writer's omitted knowledge would be underlying and felt by the reader, as would his subconscious. The importance of the subconscious, the seven-eighths of the iceberg below the surface, was instrumental to Hemingway's writing process and routine: "I learned not to think about anything that I was writing from the time I stopped writing until I started again the next day. That way my subconscious would be working on it and at the same time I would be listening to other people and noticing everything."

Hemingway's final work *The Old Man and the Sea* (1952) appears to pour with symbolism—Christ on the cross, the loss of youth, the struggle of manhood—yet to him the book was just a story about an old man, a boy, a fish, and the sea. Any symbolism was imparted through the subconscious. To Hemingway any book with preconceived symbolism "sticks out like raisins in raisin bread." "Raisin bread is all right, but plain bread is better," he said. Hemingway always strived to write "the truth": the things he cared about in the way he wanted to tell them. When hearing F. Scott Fitzgerald's admission that he changed good stories to tailor them for magazine submission, Hemingway said, "I did not believe anyone could write any way except the very best he could write without destroying his talent."

Brevity

In Hemingway's work the depth of his characters can be projected in a few words,

JOHN GILLARD

whereas a lesser writer might take a page. From *The Sun Also Rises* (1926): "Frances was a little drunk and would have liked to have kept it up but the coffee came…." If we had been told simply that Frances would have liked to continue drinking then so much would be lost. To Frances being drunk is like a persona or a façade to be "kept up." Does she enjoy this persona or is she worried that not keeping it up will reveal something fragile? She drinks to excess but is governed enough by the social convention of coffee at the end of a meal to stop. The coffee is not passive in its arrival but actively "came," as if the act was taken to stop Frances from drinking, perhaps a common tactic by those around her. We are not told and so are left to muse, just briefly, but for long enough to add to the texture of our reading.

The brevity of Hemingway's writing was initially crafted in his early writing of short stories. He continued to work further and further toward the omission of every superfluous word until the end, to the point where it often took him a full morning to write a paragraph. This makes the fact he drafted *The Old Man and the Sea* in eight weeks an all the more impressive feat of discipline. As he said, "There is nothing to writing. All you do is sit down at a typewriter and bleed."

Hemingway at home in Cuba. Behind him is a potrait of himself.

In *The Sun Also Rises* Hemingway wrote of the "lost generation" of writers and artists in Paris during the 1920s. Following the war there was a reaction against the traditional prose of prewar literature. Hemingway turned to a more brutal language of greater simplicity and brevity.

"I always worked until I had something done and I always stopped when I knew what was going to happen next. That way I could be sure of going on the next day."

—Ernest Hemingway, *A Moveable Feast*

014

HEMINGWAY'S ICEBERG

Start by writing a detailed character profile in the section of the opposite page below the water line entitled "submerged iceberg." You might imagine you are at a dinner party and describing the person sitting opposite you or maybe choose a family member. Once you have written the detailed profile, try to convey the same key observations, character traits, and backstory in only a couple of lines—enough to achieve the same sentiment, if not more, in the "exposed iceberg" space.

Exposed iceberg

Water line

Submerged iceberg

While sitting around a table with other writers Ernest Hemingway was challenged as part of a bet to write a six-word novel. He came up with: "For sale: Baby shoes, never worn." He won the bet.

Exercise: Write your own six-word story. The story needs to project a backstory and perhaps a future story. In "Baby shoes" we can see a past, a baby's death. And we see a present, selling the shoes either due to hardship or for closure.

#016 | PACE

You can control pace with sentence length and rhythm. A lot of short sentences together can feel like constant punctuation. But they can add balance to a proliferation of long sentences. Sentence length can also match action. For example, consider the sentence, "Her hand twitched." A short sentence mirrors the twitch. Observations of passing scenery on a train journey might be mirrored by long sentences.

Exercise: Choose a piece of writing you have done previously that has at least ten continuous sentences. Or write a similar-length piece describing a journey you have made. Read your writing back, paying close attention to the rhythm of the sentences and whether you linger over certain parts and stop abruptly at others. Is there a certain beat to it? Is there is a constant "stop, start" of short sentences, or no time to come up for air with numerous long sentences? Perhaps consider rewriting the piece, interchanging long and short sentences, and see the effect on pace and rhythm.

A HISTORICAL CROWD

Imagine you are in a crowd of people in a place of your
choosing, in each of the years listed below. Describe the
crowd and write down anything as dialogue that you can
hear people say or shout.

1205:

_____

_____

_____

_____

_____

_____

_____

_____

_____

1855:

_____

_____

_____

1925:

1965:

VLADIMIR NABOKOV

Born: April 22, 1899

Died: July 2, 1977

Writing: Postmodern

Key work: *Lolita*

VLADIMIR NABOKOV

V ladimir Nabokov ignited outrage with the publication of *Lolita* (1955). He paved the way for future writers to push the boundaries of what is acceptable and test society's appetite for the immoral and outrageous.

Lolita

Lolita changed the landscape of literature and perhaps even of society. The novel was first published in France in 1955 by Olympia Press, who also published William S. Burroughs's *Naked Lunch* four years later. *Lolita* created controversy and acclaim in equal measure. The book, portraying a grown man's passion for a 12-year-old girl, was subsequently banned in France, and no American or British publisher would touch it for fear of prosecution. But the overwhelming acclaim for Nabokov's writing outweighed the moral outrage, and the novel was published in the US in 1958 and in Britain in 1959. This landmark in freedom from censorship was followed in 1960 by Penguin, which overcame a legal challenge to publish *Lady Chatterley's Lover* (1928).

With *Lolita* Nabokov challenged the morality of the reader and of society. In 1956 he wrote an afterword to *Lolita*, distancing himself from responsibility for his character's moral stance. Nabokov said there is no moral to the story and the reader must be the judge. But we are given only Humbert Humbert's view by which to judge, and he is both shockingly open and highly unreliable as a narrator.

In pushing the boundaries of what was acceptable in terms of language and content, and overtly opening up a relationship between reader and text, Nabokov's novels *Lolita*, *Pale Fire*, and *Ada*, together with writers like William S. Burroughs, heralded a shift from modernism to postmodernism.

Passion for Detail

Nabokov is a master of wordplay. He uses many linguistic devices, from alliteration to onomatopoeia, in an idiosyncratic, distinctive way. In this extract from *Lolita* he relates the alliteration of words to actions, before referring to life as an alliteration: "Life with you was lovely—and when I say lovely, I

mean doves and lilies, and velvet, and that soft pink 'v' in the middle and the way your tongue curved up to the long, lingering 'l.' Our life together was alliterative…."

Nabokov related his mastery of language to his love of solving chess problems. To Nabokov the "originality, invention, conciseness, harmony, complexity, and splendid insincerity" of creating a chess problem was like the creative process of writing his books. Talking about *Lolita* he said, "She was like the composition of a beautiful puzzle—its composition and its solution at the same time, since one is a mirror view of the other, depending on the way you look."

Nabokov's trilingual upbringing (English, Russian, and French) had a profound influence on his style, harnessing the aesthetic qualities of each language. Nabokov lectured on Russian and European literature at Cornell University. He believed in the importance of style, structure, and linguistic artistry above all else. When teaching James Joyce's *Ulysses* he was more interested in the exact location of the protagonists in Dublin than the deeper issues of Irish identity and history.

Nabokov asked his family to burn his unfinished novel *The Original of Laura* on his death. The manuscript consisted of 125 index cards. This was Nabokov's usual writing method—writing drafts of his novels on a large series of cards. They were not destroyed, but kept in a Swiss bank vault. When the work came to light, it turned out to be "vintage Nabokov." His son Dmitri published the novel in 2009.

"The pages are still blank, but there is a miraculous feeling of the words being there, written in invisible ink and clamoring to become visible."

—Vladimir Nabokov

018

WORDPLAY

Vladimir Nabokov is known for the playfulness of his language. Here are three examples of his wordplay:

- "He broke my heart. You merely broke my life."
- "Do not be angry with the rain; it simply does not know how to fall upwards."
- "Lolita, light of my life, fire of my loins. My sin, my soul. Lo-lee-ta: the tip of the tongue taking a trip of three steps down the palate to tap, at three, on the teeth. Lo. Lee. Ta."

Nabokov takes words, pulls them apart, twists them, and makes something new. A broken life, rain falling upward, a sensual description of a name using the three syllables that form it.

Exercise: Describe something in an unusual way by forming an unexpected association.

| ALLITERATION

The repetition of sounds in a series of words creates rhythm and the visual similarity of the words affects the focus of the reader.

An excellent example of effective alliteration can be seen in James Joyce's *The Dead*: "His soul swooned slowly as he heard the snow falling faintly through the universe and faintly falling, like the descent of their last end, upon all the living and the dead."

Exercise: Write down some words using alliteration. Start off following Joyce's lead and then continue from there.

soul	swooned	slowly		faintly	falling
s	s	s		f	f

020

UNUSUAL COMPARISONS

Forming similes by making unusual comparisons can enlighten an image and last in the memory. Vladimir Nabokov and Haruki Murakami offer two excellent examples of this. Nabakov in *Lolita* compares leaning elderly ladies to the leaning tower of Pisa: "Elderly American ladies leaning on their canes listed toward me **like** towers of Pisa." Murakami in *Kafka on the Shore* compares an ear to a fragile mushroom: "One pointy ear peeks out from the strands of her hair **like** a little mushroom, looking strangely fragile."

Exercise: Write some similes creating an unusual comparison between two things.

WILLIAM S. BURROUGHS

Born: February 5, 1914

Died: August 2, 1997

Writing: Beat Generation; postmodern

Key work: *Naked Lunch*

W illiam S. Burroughs was a member of the Beat Generation. His novel *Naked Lunch* (1959) is a key work in Beat literature. Norman Mailer (*The American Dream*) once said, "Burroughs is the only American novelist living today who may conceivably be possessed of genius."

A Tumultuous Life

The Beat Generation was a group of highly influential writers who came together in New York following World War II. They lived, documented, and part-fictionalized the world around them—drug-fueled and full of creative and intellectual energy. They wrote about drugs, homosexuality, spirituality, death, and extreme violence, and reacted against social control and conformity.

Burroughs, together with Jack Kerouac and Allen Ginsberg, embodied Beat culture. He experimented with drugs and was addicted to heroin for most of his adult life. The fellow Beat writer, Lucien Carr, embroiled him in the murder of a childhood friend. He accidently killed his wife with a gun in a drunken game. He fled to Mexico City and lived in London, Paris, Berlin, and Tangier. *Naked Lunch*, Burroughs's second published novel, drew upon his experiences in New York and Tangier. The content of drug taking and homosexuality was so graphic and controversial that the book was initially banned in America.

Burroughs's work was experimental and key to the emergence of postmodernism. *Naked Lunch* is considered one of the first works of postmodernism. Where modernism broke literary traditions of style and form, Burroughs's work diversified into something different. *Naked Lunch* is a series of vignettes with no clear narrative structure. Burroughs stated that the chapters could be read in any order. This fragmented form mirrors the chaotic lives and society in the book. There is irony and pastiche: "Confusion hath fuck his masterpiece." He wrote in a style that Jack Kerouac described as "spontaneous prose." He observed and embraced happy accidents in the process of writing, moving away from the crafted prose of the modernists.

"'Well, it's all in a day's work,' (Dr.) Benway says, with a sigh, after a patient fails to survive heart massage with a toilet plunger."

—William S. Burroughs, *Naked Lunch*

Experimental

"and
Start
west
I can feel the heat closing in." Burroughs's opening to *Naked Lunch* has the rhythmic beat and line structure of "tick, tick, tick, boom." It is as if Burroughs is crunching his knuckles before delivering a left hook to the reader's chin. Burroughs doesn't talk in universal tones like Maya Angelou; his preoccupation is the individual. He is taken deep into his own state of mind by drugs and anti-authoritarian paranoia. He offers insights and explanations to the reader: "I can tell you in confidence he is due for a hot shot. (Note: This is a cap of poison junk sold to addict for liquidation purposes. Often given to informers. Usually the hot shot is strychnine since it tastes and looks like junk.)" There is an implicit relationship with the reader. The author is saying, "Follow me." You follow him and he turns to you occasionally with an explanation of what is happening. All the while he is walking in front of you through the streets of New York at a fast pace saying, "This is my world; keep up."

With the Nova Trilogy (1961–67), set in a nightmarish future, expanding upon the themes in *Naked Lunch*, Burroughs experimented further with his writing process. He assembled scissored fragments from the works of other writers, as well as his own manuscripts, piecing them together in random order. This method had its origins in the art movement Dadaism. T. S. Eliot, a major influence on Burroughs, had used the "found" form, splicing newspaper extracts into his poem "The Waste Land" (1922). Burroughs developed this "cut-up" method further using the work of Kafka, Eliot, Joyce, Kerouac, Shakespeare, and those he himself inspired, such as Jean Genet.

THE WILLIAM S. BURROUGHS EXERCISE

"For exercise, when I make a trip, such as from Tangier to Gibraltar, I will record this in three columns in a notebook I always take with me. One column will contain simply an account of the trip, what happened. I arrived at the air terminal, what was said by the clerks, what I overheard on the plane, what hotel I checked into. The next column presents my memories; that is, what I was thinking of at the time, the memories that were activated by my encounters; and the third column, which I call my reading column, gives quotations from any book that I take with me. I have practically a whole novel alone on my trips to Gibraltar."
—William S. Burroughs, from an interview in
The Paris Review

Exercise: Record encounters you have during a day (or days)—whether they are on holiday, at work, climbing Mount Everest—breaking them down William S. Burroughs-style. As you collect all aspects of these encounters you will build up plenty of material to work with. They may trigger an idea or turn into a piece of work. You may want to "cut up," move them about or splice them with other pieces of literature.

Account	Memories/thoughts	Quotations

#022 CUT-UPS

Pick and write down five random sentences from anywhere in this book, either from the profiles and/ or your own writing from the exercises. Mix them up and splice them together in some way to make a new, coherent paragraph.

Date

DIALOGUE CLUTTER

It is essential to avoid clutter within dialogue. It is equally important for each line of dialogue to push the action forward and/or develop character. Much of what we say in real life would be useless on the page. An extreme example to be avoided would be something like:

"How are you?"
"Not bad, you?"
"Good, thanks."

Exercise: Imagine two people bumping into each other and starting a conversation, whether it is in the street, at a wedding, a funeral, or wherever. Write dialogue between the two people, avoiding any meaningless clutter. Think about why their meeting might be less than small talk.

Date

ris Murdoch is one of the great British writers of her generation. Proudly Anglo-Irish, she became a Dame of the British Empire and was a philosophy academic at Oxford University. Her book *Under the Net* (1954) was chosen by *Time* magazine as one of the hundred best English-language novels of the twentieth century.

A Philosophical Tone

Although Murdoch did not consider her work "philosophical fiction" in the vein of Sartre or Kafka, her academic excellence in existentialism and questions of morality shine through in her work. There is certainly a philosophical tone to her prose, layered with beautiful flowing and textured language: "We are such inward secret creatures, that inwardness the most amazing thing about us, even more amazing than our reason. But we cannot just walk into the cavern and look around" (*The Sea, The Sea*; 1978). There is a layer of the philosophical, the existential, beneath the everyday language and phrasing of the prose.

Key themes in Murdoch's work are questions of human morals, the search for goodness, and the individual looking inward, following the tradition of novelists such as Dostoyevsky,

Tolstoy, and Proust. She writes about religion and Anglo-Catholic crises of faith. She looks into the individual's spiritualism, her own leaning toward Buddhism—spiritualism without a God. She wrote with humor: "Hegel says that Truth is a great word and the thing is greater still. With Dave we never seemed to get past the word" (*Under the Net*). When she talks about drugs with knowingly ironic humor, it is the antithesis of the Beat Generation attitude: "However, on one occasion, several years ago, I was idiot enough to take a dose of LSD. (I did it to please a woman.) I had what is known as a 'bad trip'" (*The Sea, The Sea*).

The Power of the Letter

In 2010 a collection of letters from Murdoch to the French Oulipo group co-founder, Raymond Queneau, were unearthed. The collection offers a fascinating insight for

aspiring writers into the sensibilities of a great writer starting out in her craft. Through their correspondences we see a writer at times filled with hatred and contempt for her prose. Murdoch is thought to have abandoned as many as six manuscripts before completing her first book. She later destroyed them. In 1947, seven years before her first published novel, she wrote to Queneau: "Work in Progress hasn't got far yet (not far enough, notably, for me to ruin it. This usually happens about Chapter IV). I will let you see it, but later (tho' I feel rather ill at the thought of you reading it)." Professor Peter Conradi, the author's official biographer, said: "Iris Murdoch's first novel has an extraordinary confidence that many first novels lack. She has this assurance because she was willing to abandon or destroy her early works."

It's always interesting to note the mode of writing of authors before computers became the norm. Murdoch wrote all of her novels by hand, correcting as she went, and gave a single copy to her publisher. She never knew how many words she had written. She never counted. Stephen King by contrast set his daily standard at 2000 words a day. Murdoch

> **"Good art, whatever its style, has qualities of hardness, firmness, realism, clarity, detachment, justice, truth."**
>
> —Iris Murdoch, Interview with *The Paris Review*

was early to bed and early to rise. She worked in the morning and wrote letters in the afternoon. There has always been a strong tradition of letter writing between authors. It was, in some part, William S. Burroughs's letters written to Allen Ginsberg that propelled him into a writing career. Murdoch's letters to Queneau were invaluable to her, and she dedicated her first novel to him.

024

THE SEA, THE SEA

Note down as many adjectives, nouns, and verbs as you can think of associated with the sea. Then look back at the words and write down any interesting word combinations that you find. This process of word generation can lead to images and ideas that may otherwise remain untapped.

Adjectives:

_____

_____

_____

_____

_____

_____

_____

_____

_____

_____

_____

Nouns:

_____

_____

_____

_____

Verbs:

Unusual combinations:

A zeugma is a sentence where multiple shades of meaning in a single word or phrase are used in relation to two other parts of a sentence.

Exercise: Write some sentences incorporating a zeugma. Is it a device that might find a place in your work? Below are some examples.

"He had been married, but his wife had left him childless and long ago..." Iris Murdoch, *The Philosopher's Pupil*

"[They] covered themselves with dust and glory."
Mark Twain, *The Adventures of Tom Sawyer*

"When I address Fred I never have to raise either my voice or my hopes." E. B. White in "Dog Training" (1940), an essay for *Harpers*

RANDOM PLACE

Find a random proper noun from a newspaper or magazine (scan articles for capital letters). Use this as an imaginary setting. What does this place look like, who lives there, and what happens there?

For example: From *The Times:* "Oettingen"—the name of a professor and could also lend itself to the name of an interesting place.

#027

"SUNLIGHT AWAITS"

Write a short piece, starting with the word "sunlight,"
ending with the word "awaits," and including in the body
of your writing the following words:

Sunlight
Fridge magnet
Venerable
Artistic
Awaits

Sunlight

awaits

Born: November 11, 1922

Died: April 11, 2007

Writing: Counter-culture; satire; sci-fi

Key work: *Slaughterhouse-Five*

K
urt Vonnegut is one of the great postwar American writers, best known for his satirical and darkly humorous novels. With a uniquely unconventional style he blends fiction, commentary, and autobiography.

An Experimental Writer

Vonnegut was raised during the Great Depression. The despairing voice and pessimistic outlook on humanity seen in much of his work may be traced back to this time. His father's business collapsed and his mother became dependent on alcohol and prescription drugs. Having been taken out of private school, Vonnegut graduated through high school and studied Biochemistry at Cornell University.

Vonnegut is often placed among the great anti-war writers. His writing was forever marked by his experiences during World War II. Captured at the Battle of the Bulge and sent to a prisoner-of-war camp, Vonnegut survived the bombing of Dresden only because of his captivity 60 feet below ground in an old slaughterhouse. This experience punctuated much of his work and inspired what is considered his masterpiece, *Slaughterhouse-Five, or The Children's Crusade:*

A Duty-Dance with Death (1969), the story of Billy Pilgrim, prisoner of war, alien-zoo exhibit, and time-traveler.

Vonnegut often played around with narratives, time-shifts, fiction, and reality— none more so than his final novel *Timequake* (1997) in which everyone and everything is sent back from 2001 to 1991, reliving the decade in a constant state of *déjà vu*. While living through the timequake himself, Vonnegut talks directly to his alter ego, tells us of his years selling short stories to weekly magazines, and shows us letter-headed paper from the Saab dealership he worked for while living in Cape Cod. Vonnegut's voice is often heard through Kilgore Trout, an out-of-print science-fiction writer who appears to be an extension of Vonnegut himself. He describes Trout as "a hobo for much of his life, he died in luxury in the Ernest Hemingway Suite of the writers' retreat Xanadu in the summer resort village of Point Zion, Rhode Island."

Recurrent themes in Vonnegut's work are the banalities of consumer culture and the destruction of the environment (*Player Piano*, 1952; *Cat's Cradle*, 1963), which have since become central to the work of writers such as Douglas Coupland and Margaret Atwood.

‹ *Cat's Cradle*, told with Vonnegut's dark, deadpan humor and irony, has become a cult classic.

Deceptive Simplicity

Despite the experimental nature of his writing, Vonnegut's sentences always remained straightforward, revealing character or advancing story. He felt that a writer should not hold back information from the reader, or take too long revealing important details. "To hell with suspense," he wrote in his eight rules for writing a short story, "readers should have such a complete understanding of what is going on… they could finish the story themselves, should cockroaches eat the last few pages." In *Slaughterhouse-Five* Vonnegut takes this a step further and tells us, at the end of the first chapter, both the opening and closing words of his novel.

In a typical piece of contradiction for Vonnegut, he goes on to say: "The greatest American short story writer of my generation was Flannery O'Connor. She broke practically every one of my rules but the first. Great writers tend to do that." This is reflected in his work, which is a mesh of contradictions: both science fiction and yet literary, dark and yet funny, classic and yet counter-culture, kind-hearted yet detached.

One literary device frequently employed by Vonnegut in his novels is the use of a short phrase that is repeated on numerous occasions throughout the work. In the case of *Slaughterhouse-Five* this phrase is "so it goes," which is used ironically in reference to death. According to Mark Feeney, writing in the *Boston Globe*, "Its combination of simplicity, irony, and rue is very much in the Vonnegut vein."

"Be a Sadist. No matter how sweet and innocent your leading characters, make awful things happen to them, in order that the reader may see what they are made of."

—Kurt Vonnegut, *Bagumbo Snuff Box: Uncollected Short Fiction*

028

EXTREME VERSIONS OF YOU

Kurt Vonnegut's alter ego, Kilgore Trout, allows him to stretch the dimensions of his own character.

Exercise: Think about your own characteristics. You have a wealth of elements and quirks that form your own character. Think of one of these elements and take it to an extreme. Create a fictional character based on an extreme version of yourself. Who are they? What is their name? What major characteristics do they have? You may have an urge to throw pistachio nutshells on the floor when you crack them open. Perhaps your character has a carpet of pistachio nutshells on their bedroom floor—what sort of character might they be? You may have a tendency to talk too much when you are nervous—your fictional character might have the same trouble when faced with a gun to the head and ordered to be silent. How would your character react to an extreme situation? Write a 300-word monologue in the voice of your "extreme version of you," placing them in, or reporting on, an extreme situation. Thinking about yourself, and building fictional characters around elements of your own character, can be a great source of inspiration.

029

DIALOGUE WITH THE FUTURE

In many of his stories Kurt Vonnegut experiments with structure by using time travel as a plot device. In *The Sirens of Titan* (1959) the main protagonist lives in the 22nd century, from where he travels into the future.

Exercise: Place yourself in one of the years listed below and imagine yourself either in a crowd of people, somebody's house, or somewhere else, speaking to somebody. Write a piece of dialogue.

2020
2100
2500
4000
100,000

030

EXPANDING DIALOGUE

Rewrite the line of dialogue shown below five times, expanding the level of detail, and perhaps changing the meaning, on each rewrite. After the final rewrite, add a line of dialogue from the other person in response.

"I've never let you down before."

For example: First expansion—"I haven't let you down since Buenos Aires."

WORD PROGRESSION

Starting underneath the word "cardiac arrest," write a continuous list of words, each word an association of the previous one, until you reach the line through the center of the page. Continue this with each of the four trigger words in each corner of the page, writing upward from the two words at the bottom of the page. Construct a sentence, long or short, containing the four words at the end of each list.

Cardiac arrest

Mountain

Ballerina

Despair

Born: March 25, 1925

Died: August 3, 1964

Writing: Southern gothic

Key work: *A Good Man Is Hard to Find*

F lannery O'Connor is considered one of the greatest American short story writers. Before her illness and early death at the age of 39 she published two important collections of short stories as well as two highly acclaimed novels.

Brevity and Elegance

O'Connor was a remarkable writer. She mixed comedy with gruesome and shocking death. She wrote with elegance and brevity. She combined tension with a sense of the profound. Robert Towers of the *New York Times* said of O'Connor's writing that "the unspoken, the unacknowledged—hangs like a shining mist over all that has been consciously intended and consciously achieved."

This was Hemingway's iceberg: her stories uncovering hidden meaning below the surface. At readings of her seminal short story *A Good Man Is Hard to Find* (1955) O'Connor explained, "like the Greeks you should know what is going to happen in this story so that any element of suspense in it will be transferred from its surface to its interior." This element of tragedy, the reader aware of a character's inevitable gruesome fate, runs throughout O'Connor's work.

O'Connor infuses her writing with comedy too. In *A Good Man Is Hard to Find* she describes the grandmother's choice of clothing for a car journey: "at her neckline she had pinned a purple spray of cloth violets containing a sachet. In case of an accident, anyone seeing her dead on the highway would know at once that she was a lady." This ongoing humor is set against a shocking conclusion when the grandmother shows kindness to an escaped convict: "'Why you're one of my babies. You're one of my own children!' She reached out and touched him on the shoulder. The Misfit sprang back as if a snake had bitten him and shot her three times through the chest."

O'Connor's descriptions of the scenery in the state of Georgia, where much of her work is set, are particularly illuminating: "the brilliant red clay banks slightly streaked with purple; and the various crops that made rows of green

O'Connor was a tentative student of William Faulkner. She said, "the presence alone of Faulkner in our midst makes a great difference in what the writer can and cannot permit himself to do. Nobody wants his mule and wagon stalled on the same track the Dixie Limited is roaring down."

‹ O'Connor with authors Robie Macaulay (center) and Arthur Koestler (left) in 1947.

> **"Anybody who has survived his childhood has enough information about life to last him the rest of his days."**
>
> —Flannery O'Connor, *Mystery and Manners: Occasional Prose*

lace-work on the ground. The trees were full of silver-white sunlight and the meanest of them sparkled."

Startling Figures

O'Connor was a devout Catholic and attended Mass daily. Religion is central to her work and it is her Christianity that pushed her fiction to ever more extreme levels of violence and immorality. O'Connor believed that what would be repugnant to a novelist with Christian concerns would be considered ordinary to her wider, more hostile audience. And so she explained, "to the hard of hearing you shout, and for the almost blind you draw large and startling figures." O'Connor's figures were very large and very startling. Her first novel *Wise Blood* (1952) was sold in brown paper bags in her hometown of Milledgeville, Georgia. T. S. Eliot seemed unsuited to reading her fiction, because, he said, his "nerves are just not strong

enough." The warped rural communities of O'Connor's world are filled with preachers and killers, bible salesmen and farmhands, conmen and Holocaust survivors.

O'Connor attended a creative writing program while doing a postgraduate course in journalism at Iowa University in 1945. Three years later she joined a New York State writing colony. It was here she wrote the short story "The Train" (1948), which would form the first chapter of her novel *Wise Blood*. When she died from lupus in 1964, at the age of 39, O'Connor was part through her third novel for which, again, she was drawing upon a number of her previously published short stories.

032

A BACKWARD-WALKING CHICKEN

At the age of five Flannery O'Connor appeared on Pathé News showing how she had taught a chicken to walk backward. This started a lifelong love of birds. O'Connor raised chickens, emus, ostriches, toucans, and peacocks. She used the motif of the peacock in many of her works.

Exercise: Write about an unusual childhood memory. Try to really get back into the moment. What words evoke the sights, the sounds, and the smells? What were your thoughts? How did you feel?

033

CHEKHOV'S GUN

In many if her stories Flannery O'Connor used "foreshadowing." This is also known as Chekhov's gun rule: "If you say in the first chapter that there is a rifle hanging on the wall, in the second or third chapter it absolutely must go off." As well as a rule to ward off red herrings, Chekhov's gun rule when employed effectively can create a "foreshadowing," giving the reader an idea of what will happen in advance. Subtle associations can add texture to writing.

Exercise: Firstly describe a major event that is going to occur in a story you may be planning or have already written (otherwise imagine an event that may occur within a story). Then associate an image with this event: an obvious example is "a shooting"—for example, a peanut-sized hole on the front of a man's T-shirt. Then write the scenario in which this associated image is contained. Finally write the sentence, paragraph, or dialogue containing this scenario to create a "foreshadowing" of events.

Major event:

Association image:

Association scenario:

Foreshadowing:

034

A TRAIN JOURNEY

In her short story "The Train" (1948), Flannery O'Connor describes what the main character, Haze, sees from the train window: "Now the train was greyflying past the instants of trees and quick spaces of field and a motionless sky that sped darkening away in the opposite direction."

Exercise: Imagine you are on a train. Describe what you see and any thoughts triggered by what you observe. Where is the train going to or leaving from? Who are the passengers? What do you see from the train's window?

Born: March 6, 1927

Died: April 17, 2014

Writing: Magical realism

Key work: *One Hundred Years of Solitude*

G abriel García Márquez is one of the most acclaimed and influential postwar writers, both in his native Colombia and internationally. He is known for his use of magical realism and themes of politics, love, and solitude.

Magical Realism

From the moment García Márquez read the first line of Franz Kafka's *The Metamorphosis*—"As Gregor Samsa awoke that morning from uneasy dreams, he found himself transformed in his bed into a gigantic insect"—he knew he wanted to write fiction. At this time he was studying to become a journalist, a role that would later influence the themes and style of his writing. This early dichotomy of Kafkaesque surrealism and journalistic reportage is reflected in García Márquez's later work.

During a trip back to his village of birth at the age of 22, García Márquez formed the basis of what would become his trademark genre—magical realism. In an interview with *The Paris Review* he remembers, "Nothing had really changed, but I felt that I wasn't really looking at the village, but I was *experiencing* it as if I were reading it." He just had to copy the words that were already there

in front of him. In a direct literary lineage García Márquez used many of the devices William Faulkner had used in his treatment of hardships in the American Deep South. García Márquez created, like Faulkner, a fictional town (Macondo) for the setting of his first novel *Leaf Storm* (1955). Like Faulkner before him, García Márquez used multiple perspectives, shifting chronology, and streams of consciousness—common elements of magical realism. García Márquez pushed the boundaries of Faulkner's folk-tales, myth, and the supernatural into the fantastical and extraordinary. García Márquez always stated that subject matter drives writing style and that Faulkner, although a major inspiration, was not a direct influence. It was this search for the right style and tone of writing for his subject matter that led him to go five years without writing, preceding what is considered his masterpiece: *One Hundred Years of Solitude* (1967).

The interior monologue techniques of James Joyce and Virginia Woolf influenced García Márquez's writing. In perhaps his most experimental novel, *Autumn of the Patriarch* (1975), García Márquez writes with long passages and very little punctuation.

‹ Márquez's most successful book, *One Hundred Years of Solitude*, has sold more than 30 million copies.

Grandmother's Storytelling

In his novel *In Evil Hour* (1962), García Márquez had moved away from the magic of Macondo and *Leaf Storm* in order to cover the realities of his nation's political struggles and brutalities. Stylistically it leaned more toward Ernest Hemingway than William Faulkner. García Márquez searched for a means of blending the magic and the brutal. He found it in the memories of his grandmother's storytelling. She would tell extraordinary stories without expression, or, as García Márquez put it, with a "brick face." And this is what García Márquez does. He blends the fantastic with the mundane and the brutal, using the same voice.

Márquez leaned on his earlier journalistic skills of giving believability to a story by describing the details and minutiae of a scene. In *One Hundred Years of Solitude* the character Remedios the Beauty is taken into the sky by a "delicate wind of light" catching the sheets she is in the process of hanging out to dry. The humdrum act of drying sheets becomes a poetic ascension to heaven as she waves good-bye "in the midst of the

"What matters in life is not what happens to you but what you remember and how you remember it."

—García Márquez, *Living to Tell the Tale*

flapping sheets that rose up with her." She ascends magically with the "beetles and the dahlias … as four o'clock in the afternoon came to an end"— an exact detail of time, based very much in the here and now. The story is followed shortly by the brutal killing of a grandfather and his grandson at the hands of a machete-wielding police corporal. This is classic García Márquez, seamlessly blurring the lines between magic and reality.

In an interview with *Playboy* in 1983, Gabriel García Márquez explained, "I say extraordinary things in an ordinary tone. It's possible to get away with ANYTHING as long as you make it believable."

In *Love in the Time of Cholera* we are introduced to an academic parrot: "...the parrot learned to speak French like an academician... he taught him the Latin accompaniment to the mass and selected passages from the Gospel according to St. Matthew...." The parrot is seemingly magically talented but we know parrots can talk, some have a very wide vocabulary, and so there are seeds of truth. Other characters in the story never question the parrot's abilities. This has the effect of leading the reader to accept the parrot's talents as believable. All the while, García Márquez describes the parrot's talents in a very ordinary tone: "He was a deplumed, maniacal parrot who did not speak when asked to but only when it was least expected, but then he did so with a clarity and rationality that were uncommon among human beings."

Exercise: Think of an person, animal, or even object who has a magical ability or who has something magical happen to them. It might be a pig that flies or a firing squad whose guns disintegrate as they are about to pull the trigger. Write a short piece describing the scene that unfolds. Stay within the realms of reality just enough for the reader to believe it could be true. Ask yourself why those pigs are flying and what occurrence might make a pig actually fly. Keep the language ordinary and give detail to enhance believability.

036

"JESUS WEPT"

"Jesus wept" is the shortest sentence in the bible. A sentence need only consist of a noun and a verb. Creating a list of nouns and verbs, ordinary and unusual, can trigger ideas, interesting images, and even an impactful, very short sentence. Note down as many nouns and verbs as you can think of and look over them to see if there are any unique combinations you may want to use.

Noun	Verb
Jesus	wept
mountains	congregate

037

WORD ASSOCIATIONS: CITIES

This word association exercise is a great way to capture the various key points of a location in a story. They can then be expanded upon when inhabited by your characters. Write down four words that you associate with the city. Then think about the location from a different angle and write down four words that are new and unexpected associations with the city. Use the blank association spaces to imagine your own location and create key associations.

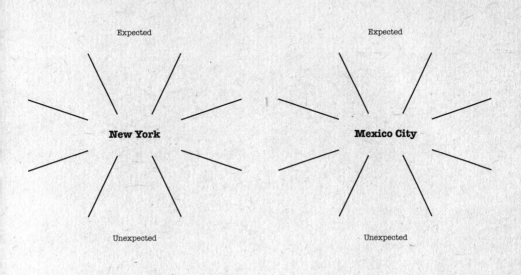

Expected

New York

Unexpected

Expected

Mexico City

Unexpected

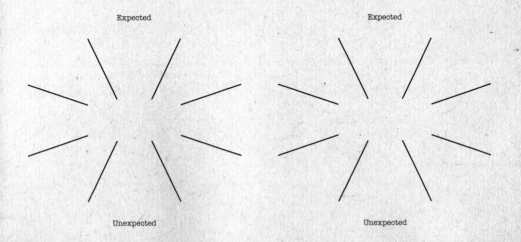

Expected

Unexpected

Expected

Unexpected

MAYA ANGELOU

Born: April 4, 1928

Died: May 28, 2014

Writing: Autobiography

Key work: *I Know Why the Caged Bird Sings*

M aya Angelou was an autobiographer, poet, dancer, screenwriter, actress, film director, honorary professor, and civil rights activist. Her book *I Know Why the Caged Bird Sings* (1969) broke new ground, challenging established ideas of what is considered autobiography.

A Universal Story

Angelou played with the scope of autobiography as a form. She attempted to tell her story as a universal story through themes of mother/child, love, loss, identity, and rising from defeat undefeated. Angelou believed autobiography should go beyond the facts of the writer's life and reach its essence: how they feel about their place in the world, the universal truths that their lives embody. She wanted to tell "the truth about the human being—what we are capable of, what makes us lose, laugh, weep, fall down, and gnash our teeth and wring our hands and kill each other and love each other."

In order to move away from simply telling the facts of her story, Angelou uses fictional devices to illuminate her work. Like a writer of fiction she takes the most intriguing and entertaining elements of three or four people from her life and merges them into one person. And her plot structures are a composite of different people's role in her life. Angelou stops short of taking these devices into the fictional-memoir realm of J. M. Coetzee's *Summertime* (2009) or Martin Amis's *Self* (1984), where real events are skewed into fiction.

Angelou follows the traditions of the slave narrative established by Frederick Douglass's *Narrative of the Life of Frederick Douglass, an American Slave* (1845) in which Frederick Douglass writes: "Once you read you will be forever free." The essence of the slave narrative was to speak for all slaves in the voice of one. This is Angelou's aim: "Had I known that the heart breaks slowly, dismantling itself into unrecognizable plots of misery... had I known yet I would have loved you…" *And Still I Rise* (1978).

‹ Maya Angelou photographed at her home in 1978, during an interview with the *New York Times*.

Angelou is speaking in the universal tone of the first person singular. Her "I" could easily be replaced by "we."

A Writing Sanctuary

Angelou wrote with a rich language, full of the melody and imagery used in the church sermons she heard and the authors she read as a child, such as James Weldon Johnson, Countee Cullen, and Edgar Allan Poe. On language Angelou said: "I love it for what it does for us, how it allows us to explain the pain and the glory, the nuances and the delicacies of our existence."

Angelou's prose is illustrative and expressive, each word earning its place on the page. She paints a picture of the way she sees the world. In *I Know Why the Caged Bird Sings* she describes the dress her mother is making for her with its "ruffles on the hem" and "cute little tucks." When she wears it, she will look "like one of the sweet little white girls who were everybody's dream of what was right with the world." Then Angelou tells us that the dress is "hanging softly over the black Singer sewing machine." The energetic rhythm slows with the dress "hanging softly," or perhaps "silently," and the word "white" significantly mirrored by "black."

Angelou lived in many places throughout her life: New York, Hawaii, and Accra, in Ghana. Wherever she lived, she would book into a hotel room to write. This was her writing sanctuary, where she could lose herself in her ideas and memories and in language. She would go there every morning at 6:30am and work for six or seven hours. The room would be cleared of almost everything except the bed she lay on to write.

"Words mean more than what is set down on paper. It takes the human voice to infuse them with shades of deeper meaning."

—Maya Angelou, *I Know Why the Caged Bird Sings*

A COMPOSITE CHARACTER

Think of three or four people you know. Write a brief description of their key character traits. Take the most interesting traits from each of them and fuse them together to form a new character. Write a character profile of your new composite character.

Person 1 characteristics:

_____

_____

_____

_____

_____

_____

Person 2 characteristics:

_____

_____

_____

_____

_____

_____

_____

_____

Person 3 characteristics:

_____

_____

_____

_____

_____

_____

_____

Person 4 characteristics:

_____

_____

_____

_____

_____

_____

_____

Composite character:

_____

_____

_____

_____

_____

_____

_____

#039 | CHILDHOOD SHOES

Write a short piece inspired by a pair of shoes you
remember from your childhood.

JOHN GILLARD

All great writers create memorable characters. Even the smallest of characters can add rich texture to a story. The following exercise offers a good starting point to create a character that might surprise.

Exercise: Write down four words that you associate with the character types below. Then think about them from a different angle and write down four words that are new and unexpected associations with the person. Use the blank association spaces to think of another character type and create key associations.

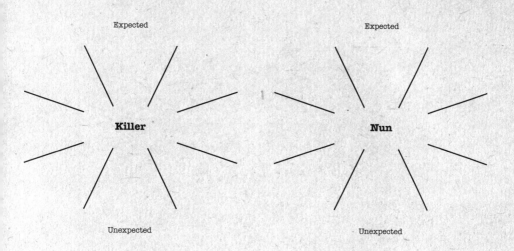

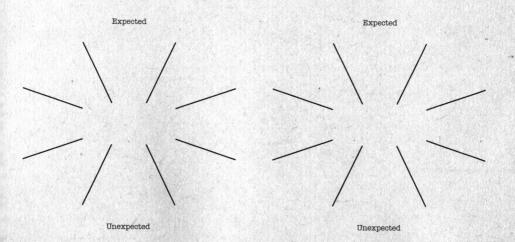

GEORGES PEREC

Born: March 7, 1936

Died: March 3, 1982

Writing: Avant-garde; existential

Key work: *La Vie mode d'emploi*

G eorges Perec is an experimental and innovative writer and member of the French writing collective, Oulipo, who place formal constraints on their writing. Perec's work *La Vie mode d'emploi* (*Life: A User's Manual*; 1978) is often cited as one of the great works of twentieth-century literature.

Set Free by Constraints

Through the course of the twentieth century the modernists had been breaking traditional literary constraints, experimenting with form and style: Woolf's interior monologues; Hemingway's brevity and infusion of the subconscious; Kafka's surrealism; Faulkner's multiple narratives. They were still, though, governed by the constraints of language. For Raymond Queneau, co-founder of the Oulipo group, "inspiration which consists in blind obedience to every impulse is in reality a sort of slavery." The impediment is the writer's blind obedience, or unknowing obedience. To the Oulipo writers, instead of attempting to break the existing constraints, they would control the constraints by forming their own. Perec, the greatest of the Oulipo writers said, "I set myself rules in order to be totally free."

The founders of the group, formed in 1960, were writers, mathematicians, and engineers. They began creating constraints such as N+7, whereby every noun in a sentence is replaced by the noun seven places forward in the dictionary. Poems were broken down into interchangeable lines, allowing one hundred billion possible readings of the poem. There were many imaginative and innovative works, but Georges Perec's stand out. He took the constraints and used them to create works that asked existential questions of human fallibility and loss.

A Void

In his novel *La Disparition* (1969), Perec uses a "lipogram" constraint: no word containing the letter "e." It is a detective story about the search for Anton Vowl. It enters the surreal when the story and the form of the novel blur. Characters avoid any

Perec wrote to the Oulipo poet Jacques Roubaud that the three writers who had provided him with his self-image were "Kafka, Kafka, and Franz Kafka." The Dada artist Marcel Duchamp (1887–1968), who paved the way for experimentations in art and literature, was a member of Oulipo.

‹ Georges Perec in 1965, at work in his office in Paris's "Latin Quarter."

mention of the letter "e," or risk demise. A clue, an encyclopedia, is discovered. It has 26 volumes, but the fifth volume is missing. Chapters are numbered from one to 26, but there is no fifth chapter. The constraint forces Perec to write in long, meandering, declarative sentences and with strings of phrases. There is surprising clarity: "A gap will yawn, achingly, day by day, it will turn into a colossal pit, an abyss without foundation, a gradual invasion of words by margins, blank and insignificant, so that all of us, to a man, will find nothing to say." The piling on of nouns, adjectives, and adverbs becomes an outpouring of energetic and unsettling prose. There is deeper meaning to the story. The missing letter "e" represents Perec's missing parents: his mother killed in Auschwitz, his father lost in battle. It is perhaps the style and mode of writing, driven by constraint, that infused the story with the deep emotions Perec felt, allowing him to tackle this existential void.

La Vie mode d'emploi (1978) is structured around a mathematical algorithm based on chess and "the Knight's tour," whereby the knight moves around the board touching each square only once. There are 100 moves.

> **"What we need to question is bricks, concrete, glass, our table manners, our utensils, our tools, the way we spend our time, our rhythms. To question that which seems to have ceased forever to astonish us."**
>
> —Georges Perec, *L'infra Ordinaire*

Perec constructs a story around a soon-to-be-demolished apartment block with ten stories and ten rooms per floor. Each chapter is set in one of the rooms. There are 99 chapters. One of the chapters is missing: the writer has failed. The main protagonist, Bartlebooth, has set himself the task of painting and then destroying 500 jigsaw puzzles, dying before his quest is complete. Perec asks us to question human fallibility and the survival of cultural artifacts: what survives and what does not? The writer who has failed in his algorithmic structure? His books?

041

PALINDROMES

A palindrome is a word, phrase, or number that reads the same backward as forward. In 1969 Georges Perec wrote a 1000-word palindrome imaginatively called *Le Grand Palindrome* (*The Big Palindrome*). An example of a palindromic sentence is the philosophical, "Do geese see God?" Palindromes are playful and can be used within a piece of writing: "My *1-2-1* with *Dr. Awkward* was palindromic from the start. Tired. Frustrated. The aroma of terrible coffee filled the room. *Did I face decaf?...I did.*"

Exercise: Write a word, sentence, passage, or longer piece of writing, incorporating a palindrome.

Date

042

A classic Oulipo writing constraint is N+7, whereby every noun in a sentence is replaced by the noun seven places forward in the dictionary.

Exercise: Write a short piece of writing on any subject you like, using any writing method you like, whether it be a first-person monologue, an account of your day, or just a simple single line of fiction. Once complete, grab a dictionary. Work through your piece replacing every noun with the noun seven places forward in the dictionary.

Once you've finished, read your writing back. How does it read? Does anything new and surprising jump out at you? Are there any new objects, ideas, or thoughts that might lead you onto another thought pattern for a new piece of writing? Or can you take your existing piece down a new direction?

Example:
"The old car salesman poured the contents of the canister over his boss's desk, covering the sales book with glistening turtle wax."

Becomes—
"The old caramel saline poured the contents of the cannibal over his botch's despot, covering the salicional boondoggle with glistening tussle wean."

043

99 PERSPECTIVES

Raymond Queneau wrote a short episode where the narrator witnesses an altercation on a bus. He then retold the same story 99 times using different styles of writing. Some of the styles Queneau used are comedy, dream, philosophical, and haiku.

Exercise: Write a short episode that has some element of story. Rewrite it three, six, nine, or 99 times in different styles. The act of rewriting may lead to something unexpected and may inspire.

Pi, the ratio of a circle's circumference to its diameter, has an intrinsic quality. The digits when transferred and played as musical notes (ie, "3" is played as a C note) play a pleasant melody. When applied to writing ("3" becomes a three-letter word), the digits of Pi can create a surprisingly good structure for a sentence. The act of writing as a problem-solving exercise based on the constraint of Pi can be very creative and offer some interesting results.

3.14159265359

Example: "Hey," I says. "I never structure or change prose." Mum winks knowingly.

If you want to keep going: 3.14159265358979323846264338327950288419716939937510582097494459230...

Born: November 18, 1939

Died: N/A

Writing: Speculative fiction

Key work: *The Handmaid's Tale*

Margaret Atwood is one of Canada's most celebrated writers. She is a prolific writer of novels, poetry, short fiction, and nonfiction. She is experimental and progressive in her writing projects.

Out of the Wilderness

As with many current writers, such as Peter Carey and J. M. Coetzee, Atwood covers a wide variety of literary genres. *Surfacing* (1972) draws upon elements of thriller, ghost story, and travelogue; *Alias Grace* (1996) is a historical novel based on a true figure in nineteenth-century history; *The Handmaid's Tale* (1985) is set in a dystopian future. In the case of *The Handmaid's Tale*, Atwood has her own name for the genre. Rather than science fiction it is "speculative fiction," meaning "a work that employs the means already to hand and that takes place on Planet Earth."

Atwood writes with brevity, precision, and elegance. In *Alias Grace* she shows in only a few words the innocent nature of the main protagonist and the seeming joy of a simple domestic task: "The shirts and the nightgowns flapping in the breeze on a sunny day were like large white birds, or angels rejoicing, although without any heads."

The flowing rhythm is jolted by her "correction" to her thought process. Atwood's humor is dark. In *The Blind Assassin* (2000) the Chase family discusses buttons: "War is good for the button trade. So many buttons are lost in a war, and have to be replaced—whole boxfuls, whole truckloads of buttons at a time. They're blown to pieces, they sink into the ground, they go up in flames."

The theme of women's status and subjugation is common in Atwood's work—from her first novel, where a recently engaged woman feels her body and mind becoming separated (*The Edible Woman*; 1969), to a possible future of sexual oppression (*The Handmaid's Tale*), and to a past, where a woman convicted of murder is either a desperate victim or innately evil (*Alias Grace*). Atwood grew up in the wilderness of northern Quebec, Canada, and experienced the increasing commercial impact of America in the 1960s and '70s. Her relationship with Canada plays an important

Atwood sees the label "science fiction" as a pejorative term when it is applied to her work. In an interview with the BBC in the UK she distanced herself from a genre of "talking squids in outer space."

‹ Margaret Atwood photographed in 1972 for an interview in the *Toronto Star*.

role in her work. In *The Handmaid's Tale* the Canadian wilderness is seen as the only escape from the oppressive republic, which was once the United States of America.

A Poetic Catalyst

Atwood is a prolific writer and, as well as her novels, has published numerous collections of short fiction and poetry. Her poetry is often a catalyst to her novels. In an interview with *The Paris Review* she describes the process: "I don't think I solve problems in my poetry; I think I uncover the problems. Then the novel seems a process of working them out." As many writers attest to, ideas begin with an image, a scene, or a voice: "Sometimes that seed is contained in a poem I've already written."

Atwood likes to complete 1000–2000 words per day. She writes the first draft of a manuscript by hand and is attentive to the pen's movement across the page. She is progressive in her outlook on the wider world of writing. She is the inventor of the Longpen, which allows a writer to sign books remotely using a computer in one city and an electronic pen in another. She is the first contributor to the Future Library Project.

> **"Never map it out. Just get into it. Jump in, like going swimming."**
>
> —Margaret Atwood, interview with *The Daily Beast*

The project runs over a period of 100 years with one writer contributing a piece of work every year, remaining unread until 2114. In Norway 1000 trees have been planted and will be cut down in 2114 to provide the paper on which the texts will be printed and read. As an active campaigner for human rights, Atwood is, at the time of writing, auctioning the naming rights for a character in one of her novels to raise money for the cause.

#045 | WASHED-UP OBJECTS

"Love blurs your vision; but after it recedes, you can see more clearly than ever. It's like the tide going out, revealing whatever's been thrown away and sunk: broken bottles, old gloves, rusting pop cans, nibbled fishbodies, bones."—Margaret Atwood, *Cat's Eye* (1988)

Exercise: Make a list of five objects or more that might be washed up on the shore of a beach. Do any of them trigger ideas for your writing?

Communicating how something feels to the touch need not always be through associated descriptive words, such as "soft skin." Making unusual associations to describe how something feels can make the sensation of touch more powerful. The description might be relating to how something else normally feels. For example, water can feel not only wet but like the touch of a loved one, a caress. In the *The Penelopiad*, Margaret Atwood writes "Water does not resist. Water flows. When you plunge your hand into it, all you feel is a caress."

Exercise: Write down a few objects or materials that you might touch. Next to this write an adjective to describe what it feels like to the touch. Then write down how it makes you feel when you touch it. Then write a sentence including a description of how it makes you feel when you touch it.

Object/material	Adjective	How it makes you feel
Water	Wet	Caressed
Wood	Smooth/rough	Belligerent

#047   FOUR SEASONS

Imagine a setting and describe the place four times,
changing each description according to the season.

Winter:

Spring:

Summer:

Fall:

THE VIEW FROM THE TOP

Write a short piece using the following line for inspiration:

"The view from the top…"

Born: February 9, 1940

Died: N/A

Writing: Fictionalized memoir; postmodern

Key work: *Disgrace*

J. M. Coetzee is one of the leading postmodern authors writing today. His prolific work covers a wide range of literary genres. He was born in South Africa but became an Australian citizen in 2006.

Deforming the Medium

Coetzee writes for an hour a day, seven days a week. He writes his work by hand in exam books from the University of Cape Town, editing them with a red pen. He writes numerous drafts: 14 versions of his Booker prize-winning novel *Disgrace* (1999), 24 versions of his novel *Slow Man* (2005).

Coetzee rarely, if ever, discusses or analyzes his work. He is often seen as a recluse in the mold of J. D. Salinger: no interviews, no presence at his two Booker Prize awards. When presented with the 2003 Nobel Prize in Literature, rather then give an acceptance speech he read a short story about the character Robinson Crusoe and its author, Daniel Defoe. The story tells of the character and his creator, who, although so close, can never meet. This is typical of the enigmatic Coetzee. He describes his brand of political thought as pessimistic anarchistic quietism. And his characters are often equally enigmatic: "If he has a last thought, if there is time for a last thought, it will simply be, so this is what a last thought is like" (*Slow Man*). He does, though, in his fictionalized memoir *Summertime* (2009) offer insight into what makes a great writer. The insight comes via a damning critique of his sometimes real, sometimes fictional character, John Coetzee: "In general, I would say that his work lacks ambition. The control of the elements is too tight. Nowhere do you get a feeling of a writer deforming his medium in order to say what has never been said before, which is to me the mark of great writing." A great writer deforms his medium, breaks the rules, in order to say something new. Again talking about John Coetzee, one of his ex-lovers, Sophie, says, "He had no special sensitivity that I could detect, no original insight into the human condition." Again through extreme self-deprecation Coetzee tells us that to create great writing is to create original insight into the human existence.

Coetzee's work spans numerous genres, among them fictionalized memoir, historical fiction, and non-nonfiction. This is in contrast to a writer such as William Faulkner, who wrote time and again about his "own little postage stamp of native soil."

‹ When Coetzee won the 2003 Nobel Prize in Literature, he became the second South African to be honored.

Disgrace and Brutality

Coetzee's writing is clear, to-the-point, and often brutal: "I undress her, I bathe her, I stroke her, I sleep beside her—but I might equally well tie her to a chair and beat her, it would be no less intimate" (*Waiting for the Barbarians*; 1980). He creates characters that are thrown into despair, disgrace, and brutality. A man relaxing into old age has his leg amputated following a terrible cycling accident (*Slow Man*), a woman is gang-raped in post-apartheid South Africa (*Disgrace*), his alter-ego, John Coetzee, is disgraced and deported from America back to South Africa (*Summertime*). In *The Master of Petersburg* (1994) Coetzee fictionalizes the character of Fyodor Dostoyevsky and places him in a state of turmoil, grief-stricken by the death of his stepson.

Coetzee writes largely in the present tense, which gives his prose gripping immediacy. He opens sentences with key words, even if it means the sentence jars: "The joys of possession I have never felt very acutely" (*Diary of a Bad Year*; 2007). "The joys of possession" is what grabs our attention and drives the sentence. Again, in *Elizabeth Costello* (2003): "Jokes, secrets, complicities;

> ## "A book should be an axe to chop open the frozen sea inside us."
>
> —J. M. Coetzee, *Summertime*

a glance here, a word there: that is their way of being together, of being apart." He uses this device to great effect, giving emphasis to meaning. In his fictionalized-memoir trilogy he plays with narratives. In the first two volumes *Boyhood* (1997) and *Youth* (2002) he writes in the third person, with the events closely matching his life. In the third and final volume he reveals the protagonist's identity as John Coetzee, only to kill off the character and complete his story through the voices of ex-lovers being interviewed by a fictional biographer, Mr. Vincent.

Look at some of your previous work or a novel you have read. Are there any sentences that could be more gripping? Where emphasis on key words might drive the sentence and make it more illuminating? Could the reworking of a key sentence within a paragraph illuminate the paragraph? Below are two sentences from novels by J. M. Coetzee. The sentences labeled "standard" have been rewritten in a more conventional form and are followed by the original line by Coetzee. Add a couple of examples of your own on the opposite page.

Standard:

"Don't cut short these thought patterns of yours," he said. "Follow your thoughts and feelings through to their end. Do this and you will grow with them."

Coetzee:

I urge you: don't cut short these thought-trains of yours. Follow them through to their end. Your thoughts and your feelings. Follow them through and you will grow with them.

Standard:

Their way of being together, and of being apart, is through jokes, secrets, and complicities, a glance here, a word there.

Coetzee:

Jokes, secrets, complicities; a glance here, a word there: that is their way of being together, of being apart.

Elizabeth Costello is a recurring character in the work of J. M. Coetzee and is one of his alter egos. Coetzee shows great skill in writing from the female perspective. Writing from the perspective of a character of the opposite sex and finding a truly representative voice is a very important, yet difficult, skill.

Exercise: Write an account of a small episode where you hail a taxi but as you are getting in another person pushes past you and gets in. The taxi drives off. Describe what happens and what you are thinking. Does the other person say anything? If so, what do they say and how do they sound? Do you say anything? Then flip the sex of the two protagonists around and rewrite the episode from the point of view of somebody of the opposite sex. Do the nuances of language change? Does the episode change in any way?

RANDOM TITLE

Look in a newspaper or magazine to find a random title for a short piece of writing. For example, this from *The Times*: "A short walk across Fox Plaza."

PETER CAREY

Born: May 7, 1943

Died: N/A

Writing: Historical fiction; postmodern

Key work: *True History of the Kelly Gang*

P eter Carey is one the foremost writers of Australia. His work spans a wide range of literary genres and styles. *True History of the Kelly Gang* (2000) is an important document of national identity, giving a voice to a national icon.

Building Little Sheds and Huts

Carey did not find instant success when he first started to write novels. It was only when he turned from writing his early, unpublished novels to the short story form that he believes something clicked. "When I first set out to be a writer I had no real interest in character and certainly no aptitude or ability to create character," he said in an interview for *The Paris Review*. This is from a writer who is known for his deeply rich and witty characters and prose. "I had been trying to build grand palaces, and now I was building little sheds and huts." It was only when he began to read daily and practice writing short stories week after week that he truly began to learn his craft. It was from a short story that his first published novel evolved, *Bliss* (1981).

In Carey's early work the seeds of ideas came from images. He would have a clear picture of where the book would end, and then consider how the story would arrive at this point. This approach was used to great effect in the first of his Booker Prize-winning novels, *Oscar and Lucinda* (1988). He weaves together 111 micro-chapters to reach the image of a glass church floating down the river, his starting point.

Tearing and Disrupting

In his later works the seeds are voices, telling stories: the strong Irish voice of Ned Kelly (*True History of the Kelly Gang*); the Australian pitch and profanities of Michael "Butcher" Boone in *Theft: A Love Story*. In listening to these voices Carey rips out the punctuation and shakes up the grammar. This allows the dialogue to flow, giving rich character to the voices: "… after we ate we was silent on our blankets looking out across the mighty Great Divide I never seen this country before it were like a fairy story landscape…" (*True History of the Kelly Gang*). Carey finds this "ability to disrupt and tear

True History of the Kelly Gang has parallels with the work of the influential modernist William Faulkner: the parochial voice of characters, long sentences with minimal punctuation, and the blurring of history and myth.

‹ Peter Carey at home in New York in 2007.

sentences" liberating. Lines flow from one to the next without jarring or breaking their rhythm.

Carey writes in the mornings for up to three hours. He then goes to lunch. Redrafting is an important process to him. His novels are layered with the weight of redrafting: honing characters, themes, and story. He polishes each chapter before going on to the next but is always ready to go back to the beginning and redraft if the book feels off-track. This process of redrafting often leads to pivotal moments in the evolution of his stories. Herbert Badgery, the main character in *Illywhacker* (1985), was initially going to die and fade from the story, but Carey found he liked him so much he didn't want him to go. And so Badgery became the 139-year-old man the book centers upon. He is the narrator and the living incarnation of Australia, spanning three generations.

Carey's writing is varied and eclectic. Each novel is very different from the last: moving from a story set in mythical nations (*The Unusual Life of Tristan Smith*; 1994) to the retelling of *Great Expectations* (*Jack Maggs*; 1997), from a semi-memoir set in Japan

"I started to read. I read all sorts of things in a great huge rush. James Joyce and Graham Greene and Jack Kerouac and William Faulkner, week after week."

—Peter Carey

(*Wrong About Japan*; 2006) to a story starting in current-day America and moving to a commune in 1970s Australia (*His Illegal Self*; 2007). He writes about loss and pessimism and blends it seamlessly with wit: "I had been slaughtered, legless, trolleyed, slashed, shredded, plastered, polluted, pissed. I thought, I do love my country's relationship with alcohol. How would I ever exist in the United States? I suppose I would have grief counseling instead" (*The Chemistry of Tears*; 2012).

#052 CAREY SIMILES

Peter Carey is an avid and adept user of the simile. Below are three Carey similes, repeated twice. In the first four lines the similes have been left out.

Exercise: Read and complete the line with your own simile. Be as imaginative as you like. At the bottom of the opposite page are the completed Carey similes. Compare them with yours or use them for inspiration. Can you improve on Carey's offerings?

The hair... that frizzy nest which grew outwards, horizontal like

He were still smiling but his voice were hard as

A cormorant broke the surface, like

...the hair... that frizzy nest which grew outwards, horizontal like *a wind-blown tree in an Italianate painting.*
(*Oscar and Lucinda*)

He were still smiling but his voice were hard as *a spoon rattling in a metal cup.*
(*True History of the Kelly Gang*)

A cormorant broke the surface, *like an improbable idea tearing the membrane between dreams and life.*
(*Oscar and Lucinda*)

Thinking of names for characters, places, shops, restaurants, etc in your writing can be both difficult and fun. A name can offer the reader an immediate impression of a character or place.

Exercise: Collect interesting names here: people you meet, places you visit, towns you read in the newspaper, nicknames, pet names... Use this page of the notebook to record them.

Think of a room from your childhood home. Close your eyes and visualize the room. Think about the look of it, the sound of it, and, if smoke from your granddad's pipe drifted into your bedroom, perhaps the smell of it. Write a description of the room.

DIALOGUE WITH HISTORY

Look up an event that happened in the decades listed below. Place yourself in the year of the event and imagine yourself either in a crowd of people, somebody's house, or somewhere else, speaking to somebody. Try to convey a sense of the time. Does the decade or placement of the event change the way the person speaks? Write a short piece of dialogue next to each decade.

1690s

1870s

1910s

1980s

Born: September 21, 1947

Died: N/A

Writing: Horror; gothic; sci-fi

Key work: *The Shining*

S tephen King is one of the most widely read and prolific authors of his generation. His books, often dismissed as pulp fiction by critics, show an often-underrated craftsmanship. He is at the forefront of the modern horror genre and in the mold of the classic storyteller.

What If?

King creates a scenario, fills it with characters, and then makes bad things happen to them. He tells these stories of horror, suspense, the macabre and fantastical with simple language and structures. His work blends the gothic and grotesque with real-world locations. He has a simple stylistic approach, which leaves room for the reader to paint their own picture of a scene or character, intensifying the suspense or horror where overly elaborate prose may not.

King is a prolific generator of ideas. He starts with a seed of an idea and layers the story to reach a climactic end. These layers twist and turn and evolve with the characters. His stories are rarely, if ever, plot-driven. He uses "what if" scenarios. What if a young mother and her son became trapped in their stalled car by a rabid dog? (*Cujo*; 1981). He brings together two disparate subjects like adolescent bullying and telekinesis (*Carrie*; 1974). He uses film as inspiration. *Wolves of the Calla* (2003) is based on Akira Kurosawa's film, *Seven Samurai*, in which seven samurai (or gunslingers—*The Magnificent Seven*) are hired by farmers to defend a town against bandits stealing crops. In King's story the bandits steal children. In his book, *On Writing: A Memoir of the Craft* (2000) King describes having ideas in the shower, in the car, on walks, and while dreaming on a flight to London.

The Toolbox

On Writing mixes autobiography with clear, simple advice for aspiring writers. King uses the analogy of writing as carpentry. He talks about the writer's "toolbox" in which to keep all the nuts and bolts, like vocabulary, whether vast or small, but never forced or stretched. He points to Ernest Hemingway as an example of simple words building big

King's work shows elements of the Southern gothic of William Faulkner. King, like Faulkner, takes the horror and the grotesque of classic gothic without the romanticism and sets them largely in his home state of Maine, just as Faulkner set many of his stories in Mississippi.

‹ The Stanley Hotel in Colorado. Stephen King wrote much of *The Shining* during a stay there.

houses: "He came to the river. The river was there" (*Big Two-Hearted River*; 1925).

King draws from the book *Elements of Style* (1954) by William Strunk Jr and E. B. White (*Charlotte's Web*). He champions some fundamental rules cited in this style manual: make every word count; omit needless words; action and dialogue should establish emotion, not an adverb. King is a believer in keeping to the simple dialogue attribution of "said." "'Shut up,' she urged forcefully" would never be seen in a King novel.

When King writes he keeps in mind his "ideal reader"—a single person he envisages reading the words he is writing as he is writing them, giving him perspective when engrossed in his first draft. In his case it is his wife, Tabitha. This approach is in contrast with other writers. Gabriel García Márquez said, "I no longer know whom of the millions of readers I am writing for; this upsets and inhibits me." William Faulkner was dismissive: "I have no time to wonder who is reading me. I don't care about John Doe's opinion on my or anyone else's work."

> **"If you want to be a writer, you must do two things above all others: read a lot and write a lot."**
>
> —Stephen King, *On Writing: A Memoir of the Craft*

King weaves his stories and characters with clear and simple prose. Peter Carey tears up sentences and James Joyce writes without punctuation. What they all have is a sound knowledge of fundamental rules, whether they choose to break them or not. *On Writing* and *Elements of Style* are essential reading for any aspiring writer.

Think of your own "What If?" scenarios to generate story ideas. Below are some from Stephen King, as described in *On Writing*, to start you off...

What if a policeman in a remote Nevada town went berserk and started killing everyone on sight?
(*Desperation*)

What if vampires invaded a small New England village?
(*Salem's Lot*)

What if a cleaning woman suspected of a murder she got away with (her husband) fell under suspicion for a murder she did not commit (her employer)?
(*Delores Claiborne*)

What if...

JOHN GILLARD

What if...

What if...

What if...

RANDOM WORDS, PHRASES, AND IDEAS…

Use this space in the notebook to write down anything you want that pops into your head at any time. Just as Stephen King wrote the idea for his novel *Misery* on an American Airlines cocktail napkin after waking from a dream mid-flight.

FIVE "WHYs"

Try this method of story generation. You start with a final event and ask why this event has occurred. Answer the question with "because...." Then ask "why" again and continue the process until you have asked five "why's." Have you worked your way back to an opening point in the story? Every time you write an answer to a "why" you are likely to find a character emerging. You will end up having formed a number of characters and the basic structure of your story. You can then begin writing, letting all your skills and talents flow, and allowing the characters to add texture to the story. Your characters will likely take you down different alleyways and pathways adding layers to your story. You may want to use this method to generate episodes within a story, interweaving a number of episodes to reach a final conclusion.

Final event of the story:

_____

_____

_____

_____

Why #1:

Because:

_____

_____

_____

Why #2:

Because:

Why #3:

Because:

Why #4:

Because:

Why #5:

Because:

059

PLANNING

If you are writing longer pieces of work, perhaps preparing for or writing a novel, planning will be very important. Without consideration to planning, a story can easily start off-track, with backstory becoming the main focus of the plot.

It is important to have an idea of overall structure with an impactful beginning, middle, and end. You may have three key, memorable events but they all appear later in the story. Is there a case for moving the starting point? Opening with that first impactful scene? Bringing the second impactful scene to the middle, leaving the third for a climactic ending? The backstory can then be revealed along the way, adding texture to the story and characters, and the weight of omission (see Hemingway's Iceberg, page 46).

Exercise: Use the following to review the structure of your story ideas. On the left, list very brief details of the key events in your story. From these, pick out the three most impactful events in the story and put the first under "beginning," the second under "middle," and the last under "end." Does the story still begin and end where you are expecting or does this process offer any alternative perspectives on the structure?

Key events

Beginning
(Memorable event 1)

Middle
(Memorable event 2)

End
(Memorable event 3)

HARUKI MURAKAMI

Born: January 12, 1949

Died: N/A

Writing: Magical realism; surrealism

Key work: *Kafka on the Shore*

Haruki Murakami is often cited as one of the finest living writers. He is one of a number of Japanese writers, including Banana Yoshimoto, who have been translated into many languages.

An Epiphany at the Baseball

Two epiphanies have been key to the life and work of Murakami. The first came in 1978, at the age of 29, while sitting on a grass verge outside the Jingo baseball stadium in Tokyo. With little writing experience he decided there and then he would write a novel. *Hear the Wind Sing* was published the following year. In 1982, having sold his jazz club to dedicate himself to his writing, Murakami had his second epiphany. He would give up his 30-a-day smoking habit and go running. This epiphany, as he says in his memoir *What I Talk About When I Talk About Running* (2008), led to a remarkable period of productivity that resulted in a series of novels, bringing him critical acclaim both in Japan and internationally.

Running is one of the key ingredients in Murakami's strict writing routine. He wakes up early and writes for several hours before going for a run. He then spends his afternoons translating classic Western literature, such as *The Great Gatsby* (1925) and *The Catcher in the Rye* (1951), into Japanese. As he says, "Exerting yourself to the fullest within your individual limits: that's the essence of running, and a metaphor for life—and for me, for writing as a whole." Murakami believes repetition and routine allows imagination to flourish. In an interview with John Freedman (*How to Read a Novelist*), he describes how his ideas make their way onto the page: "It's like going into a dark room. I enter that room, open that door, and it's dark, completely dark. I can see something, and I can touch something and come back to this world, this side, and write it." What he often finds are characters far from the regimented "normal" nature of his routine—a psychic hired to find a missing cat (*The Wind-up Bird Chronicle*; 1994), ageless World War II soldiers (*Kafka on the Shore*; 2002), a man who believes a giant frog is taking over Tokyo (*After the Quake*; 2000).

JOHN GILLARD

Before his epiphanies Murakami says he had never created anything; afterward, creativity spewed out of him.

Inevitable Solitude

In 1995 the Kobe earthquake and the terrorist sarin-gas attack on the Tokyo underground led to a shift in Murakami's writing. He returned to Japan, having lived in America since the late 1980s, and spent a year listening to survivors' stories. During this time he says he began to "tap into the darkness found in society and history," rather than the individual darkness of his early work. Either way, as a writer Murakami has to embrace, cope with, and harness the inevitable solitude as he opens the door to that dark room—"…this sense of isolation, like acid spilling out of a bottle, can unconsciously eat away at a person's heart and dissolve it."

Murakami mixes humor with darkness, the mundane with the fantastic, the real with the surreal. He blends stark biological detail with the ethereal: "Somewhere in his body— perhaps in the marrow of his bones—he would continue to feel her absence." (*Blind Willow, Sleeping Woman: 24 Stories*; 2006).

"There aren't any new words. Our job is to give new meanings and special overtones to absolutely ordinary words."

—Haruki Murakami, "Jazz Messenger"

He writes about memories and the essence of human existence: "Body cells replace themselves every month. Even at this very moment. Almost everything you think you know about me is nothing more than memories" (*A Wild Sheep Chase*; 1982). He writes about love in all its shapes and forms, often using the surreal to illustrate it: "'How much do you love me?' Midori asked. 'Enough to melt all the tigers in the world to butter,' I said" (*Norwegian Wood*; 1987).

#060 MURAKAMI METAPHOR

In *The Wind-Up Bird Chronicle* Haruki Murakami uses metaphor to describe loneliness: "The pages of a book in my hands would take on the threatening metallic gleam of razor blades." Murakami gives the book a sinister edge with the unexpected association of page and razor blade.

Exercise: Think of an everyday object, perhaps a door, and create a metaphor that will make the door more sinister, associating it with loneliness, or anger, or despair. Then write a sentence using this metaphor to bring out strong emotion.

Door — _____

Sentence:

ONOMATOPOEIA

When spoken aloud onomatopoeic words imitate the sound they are describing. This enables the reader to "hear" what is happening and can bring them further into the writer's world. Onomatopoeic words fall into five categories relating to water, air, collisions, voice, and animals. Here are some examples:

Ernest Hemingway, *For Whom the Bell Tolls*: "He saw nothing and heard nothing but he could feel his heart pounding and then he heard the clack on stone and the leaping, dropping clicks of a small rock falling."

Haruki Murakami, *Kafka on the Shore*: "Her earrings jiggle back and forth..."

Exercise: Write some onomatopoeic words relating to each of the five categories below. Then create a sentence using one or more of the words you have written.

Water: _____

_____

_____

_____

Air:

Collisions:

Voice:

Animals:

Does a narrator have to be a person?

Exercise: Try writing from the perspective of a building, a boat, or a tree. Let them describe as a first-person narrator the things that go on around them. What have they witnessed in their history? What people have lived or died in the building? Has the tree witnessed emotional moments that have long since passed?

WORLD RECORDS

Writing the fantastical in mundane tones is one of the marks of magical realism. Make up some world records that might appear in the *Guinness Book of Records*. Think of extremes: the smallest, tallest, highest... Write about the records and the people, actions, and things involved as if they are facts.

| **Born:** March 26, 1949 |
| **Died:** N/A |
| **Writing:** Magical realism; existentialism |
| **Key work:** *Perfume: The Story of a Murderer* |

P atrick Süskind became the enigmatic *wunderkind* of German literature with the publication of his first novel *Perfume* (1985), before withdrawing from the literary scene. He has not written a novel since 1996, yet his work remains "unique in contemporary literature" (*Le Figaro*).

Literary Tradition

Süskind grew up in a small Bavarian village and studied Medieval and Modern History at the University of Munich before moving to Paris. After early success as a playwright and screenwriter he wrote his first novel, *Perfume: The Story of a Murderer*. The novel opens in eighteenth-century Paris and weaves its way through medieval villages, and rural and mountainous landscapes. As well as the incredibly textured language used to describe scents, *Perfume* shows the extent of the writer's research into a single subject: in this case, the techniques and ingredients of perfume making.

Süskind's opening description of Paris through its putrid smell is as astonishing as it is grotesque. After two pages of relentless description—"…of rotting teeth, sour milk and tumorous disease"—Süskind introduces the main character, Grenouille, who has a supernatural sense of smell but no odor. Süskind writes about solitude following in the German literary tradition of Goethe (*The Sorrows of Young Werther*; 1774) and Thomas Mann (*The Magic Mountain*; 1924). Grenouille spends many years living in a cave with time seeming not to pass.

Grenouille is torn between his feelings of greatness and his lack of odor, which renders him irrelevant and anonymous to others. Narration is in the third person omniscient but with hints of Grenouille's inner feelings and thoughts. The lines between narrator and main protagonist—the outside world and the inner mind of the individual—are blurred. This is common in Süskind's work and points to underlying philosophical questions about the human condition. In *Perfume* he poses questions about free will: Are our feelings toward others based on conscious decisions, or are we influenced by subconscious

Süskind covers a number of literary elements and influences: from gothic to magical realism, existentialism to historical fiction; from Kafka to Oscar Wilde and Camus to Thomas Mann. Despite this, Süskind claims he remembers little about the books he has read.

‹ Süskind explores the human condition, drawing largely on the works of Albert Camus (pictured on the right).

prejudices? Süskind explores the psychology that leads his alienated antihero to become a serial murderer.

Reclusive

Like Gabriel García Márquez, Süskind uses magical realism, blending historical reality with the fantastic. He writes in the style of classic historical novels such as Dumas's *The Three Musketeers* (1844). This makes the idea of a supernatural sense of smell and lack of odor, though bizarre, all the more believable. The book's narrative is entirely odor-infused. Inanimate objects are described in detail through their scent. We are placed fully in Grenouille's world.

Another common feature of Süskind's work is the outsider, in the vein of Albert Camus. In his novella *The Pigeon* (1987), the central character, Jonathan Noel, lives in solitude in order to cope with life. He follows a monotonous routine in a small apartment he has rented for 30 years. One morning he comes across a pigeon outside his apartment door, which triggers a breakdown, forcing him to question the meaning of his whole existence. Süskind uses the Kafkaesque suggestion of complexities below the surface of the mundane. The pigeon represents the inevitable reality of life: "…a pigeon is the epitome of chaos and anarchy, a pigeon that whizzes around unpredictably, that sets its claws in you, picks at your eyes…." Süskind's characters are inconsequential to the world around them, yet their feelings permeate the entire world: "…the self-loathing dammed up inside him spilled over and gushed out… flooding the outside world as perfect, vulgar hate."

In a case of life imitating art, Süskind has withdrawn from the literary scene. He lives a reclusive life, never giving interviews or accepting any public recognition for his success.

"Thousands of hours of my childhood and my youth and my manhood spent reading, and nothing is retained except a great forgetting."

—Patrick Süskind: *Amnesia in Litteris*

#064 SCENT

Bringing the senses into a piece of writing can illuminate descriptions of scenes and characters. Descriptions of sounds, tastes, and smells will draw the reader into the world you are creating. Patrick Süskind takes this to an extreme by infusing everything with elaborate descriptions of smell.

Exercise: Describe an everyday object or a place primarily through its smell. Be as detailed and precise as possible.

#065 EXPERTS

Next time you go for a latte, watch how the barista prepares it. There seems to be a lot of tapping of implements and precision pouring of milk to create leaflike shapes on the top of the coffee. How about asking the barista exactly where the coffee beans are from? If you are able to have a prolonged conversation with them, or any expert on any subject, note the details of their expertise. Precise details add texture to prose. A Nicaraguan coffee bean is far more interesting than a coffee bean.

Exercise: Record details of an expert's skills here: the names of implements they use, the adjectives they use to describe their skills, their movements.

LITERAL MEANINGS

Thinking of literal meanings for things can offer some interesting descriptions, making them more memorable. The way the German language is constructed at times has a charming simplicity that can be a good source of inspiration. In German a "slug" is a *nacktschneke*, which translates as "naked snail."

Exercise: Write down objects, materials, places, people (occupations) and give them literal meanings.

A book	is literally a	word holder
A _____	is literally a	_____

D ouglas Coupland is a prolific writer, visual artist, sculptor, furniture designer, and screenwriter. His novels capture the zeitgeist of his generation and the term "Generation X" has entered the English vernacular.

The Minutiae of Modern Life

A brief look at Coupland's website shows that he is clearly not just a novelist. We see pictures of publicly displayed sculptures, art installations, and graphic design. Coupland is a creative. His novels follow an approach of experimentation and playing around with structure, perhaps liberated by his art. *All Families are Psychotic* (2001) is written almost entirely in dialogue. *Life After God* (1994) is written almost entirely without dialogue and told through a patchwork of character monologues. It also contains handdrawn sketches for each part of the patchwork.

Coupland's work reads like well-structured streams of consciousness. His prose flows beautifully as a result, while gripping the reader with wit, angst, and the minutiae of modern life: "Maybe I'll get drunk and go shopping on eBay at eleven at night, and maybe I'll buy all kinds of crazy crap I won't remember I bid on in the morning, like a ten-pound bag of mixed coins from around the world or a bootleg tape of Joni Mitchell performing at the Calgary Saddledome in 1981" (*The Gum Thief*; 2007)

Coupland examines religion, loneliness, pop culture, and the bombardment and sensory assault of the Internet-era world. A Coupland design piece states "I miss my pre-internet brain." "Remember how, back in 1990, if you used a cellphone in public you looked like a total asshole? We're all assholes now" (*Jpod*; 2006). The other central theme that runs through his work is the examination of the human condition. You get the sense that by reading a Coupland novel you will be that little bit closer to the meaning of what it is to be human by the end. His characters muse over their own existence: "I think Christmas is about that point where we as humans split off from the rest of the Universe and become prisoners of ourselves…" (*The Gum Thief*). The use of a religious holiday, and the buying

> **"On some days the words might not come, but you have to put yourself in a time and place where they can visit you."**
>
> —Douglas Coupland, writing for litreactor.com

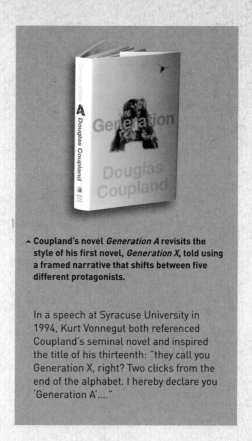

▲ Coupland's novel *Generation A* revisits the style of his first novel, *Generation X*, told using a framed narrative that shifts between five different protagonists.

In a speech at Syracuse University in 1994, Kurt Vonnegut both referenced Coupland's seminal novel and inspired the title of his thirteenth: "they call you Generation X, right? Two clicks from the end of the alphabet. I hereby declare you 'Generation A'...."

of presents in a globalized drugstore on Christmas Eve, to comment on our existence is typical Coupland—pop culture and the human condition.

Notebooks and Silence

Coupland's early work was constructed from intricate observations made in notebooks. His first novel, *Generation X*, was handwritten on loose-leaf notepaper. The importance of notetaking is offered in *Life After God*: "And if we were to collect these small moments in a notebook and save them over a period of months we would see certain trends emerge from our collection—certain voices would emerge that have been trying to speak through us. We would realize that we have been having another life altogether; one we didn't even know was going on inside us." The little things we observe in life can lead to big ideas and big stories. Stories can spring and evolve from the making of notes.

Coupland describes his writing routine as a formula. His formula is to get up when his body clock tells him to and write for a precious two hours when his creativity is at its height. He describes himself as a vampire when it comes to sleeping patterns. He goes to bed at 2am and wakes up about 10.30am. Unlike Peter Carey who always stops for lunch, Coupland never does. It would eat into his creative time. He writes every day, in silence, at his desk. His formula certainly works: He is one of the great living writers and prolific, with a new book almost every other year as well as his numerous artistic projects.

067

STREAM OF CONSCIOUSNESS

Douglas Coupland delves into the details of thoughts and the minutiae of observations. He writes the stream-of-conscious thoughts of his characters. To most effectively tap into stream of consciousness, it is important to throw off any shackles and let your pen write freely (or fingers on a keyboard). It is a great way to return from "writer's block." It usually offers up some interesting ideas, observations, and even characters, themes, and stories that may have remained un-mined. The hardest line to write is always the first. There can be anxiety over the first line, with creativity yet to kick in. The key is to just start writing. Write anything, good or bad, ugly or stylish. You can always discard the beginning anyway. What may help is to have some trigger words to get started.

Exercise: Below are some trigger words from the work of Douglas Coupland. Take one, two, or all and start writing about them until you reach the end of the next page. Then breathe, and look back at what you have written. There are likely to be some gems in there.

The Internet, notebooks, space shuttle,
Christianity, Coca-Cola

068

EARTH SANDWICH

In Douglas Coupland's novel, *Generation A* (2009), a character makes an "Earth sandwich." She places a piece of bread on the ground, having made arrangements for somebody to do the same at the exact opposite end of the earth using GPS coordinates. It's like the well-traveled thought of what would happen if every person in the world jumped up and down at the same time. What if someone made this happen?

Exercise: Can you think of any similar ideas that might find their way into a piece of your writing? Note down any ideas you have.

069

FOUND WORDS

Grab a magazine or newspaper. Randomly highlight words without any consideration (don't choose the words; keep it random). Stop when you have highlighted around 50. Discard ordinary words and keep words of substance. Write down on this page of the notebook ten words you have gathered together. Now write a paragraph, a long sentence, some dialogue, whatever you like, including all of these words.

070

LIFE AFTER...

Douglas Coupland wrote a collection of vignettes pieced together under the collective title *Life After God*. He explores interpretations of faith in a generation raised without religion. Continuing the line "Life after...," write about something that might be lost or forgotten, or about something else completely.

IMAGE CREDITS

Page

16:   © Creative Commons | Ricardo André Frantz

29:   © Print Collector | Getty Images

39:   © Print Collector | Getty Images

66:   © Getty Images

76:   © Creative Commons | Nataraja

77:   © Creative Commons | Oliver Spalt

103: © Culture Club | Getty Images

131: © Hulton-Deutsch Collection | Corbis

138: © Hulton Archive | Springer

155: © Loomis Dean | Getty Images

162: © Fred Stein | Getty Images

163: © Fred Stein | Getty Images

174: © Jean-Pierre Fouchet | Getty Images

175: © Mansell | Getty Images

182: © Duncan Rawlinson | Creative Commons

183: © Lee Lockwood | Getty Images

All other images in this book are in the public domain.